PREGNANCY AS A DISEASE

DONALD H. MERKIN

PREGNANCY as a DISEASE

THE PILL IN SOCIETY

National University Publications
KENNIKAT PRESS   //   1976
Port Washington, N. Y.   //   London

Manufactured in the United States of America

Published by
Kennikat Press Corp.
Port Washington, N.Y./London

Library of Congress Cataloging in Publication Data

Merkin, Donald H.
    Pregnancy as a disease.

    (National university publications)
    Bibliography: p.
    Includes index.
    1. Oral contraceptives—Social aspects. 2. Oral contraceptives—Side effects. 3. Diethylstilbestrol. 4. Drugs—Laws and legislation—United States. I. Title.
    [DNLM: 1. Contraceptives, Oral. 2. Diethystibestrol—Adverse effects. WP630 M563p]
RG137.5.M45   613.9'432   76-12971
ISBN 0-8046-9138-X

CONTENTS

LIST OF TABLES

FOREWORD

The Gift Relationship—from Human Blood to Social Policy by Richard Titmuss was published in 1970. This was a book of great interest and importance. In form it was a case study dealing with the provision of blood for transfusion. Written by a sociologist, the book was set in a very broad frame of reference. Titmuss provided a most perceptive analysis of the medical, economic, legal, political as well as the social factors involved in the giving and selling of a commodity as essential as human blood. This was a new kind of publication and it soon became a top seller.

The parallels between that case study and Dr. Donald Merkin's *Pregnancy as a Disease* are striking. The humane philosophy of both authors is very evident. Although the reader will sense the strong emotional involvement in the issues discussed, in neither case do the authors allow rhetoric unsupported by scientific or sociological evidence to carry them too far. Both use a common medical treatment as their vehicle for examining very basic societal values and practices.

The present book, also a case study, this time involving the oral contraceptive pill, deserves the widest readership. It will be of interest to the academic world and to professionals from many disciplines, but I suspect it will appeal broadly also to the educated public. It uses issues related to the "pill" to examine in a scholarly but highly readable way many topics which in one way or another touch us all.

This book is the first intensive review and analysis of the social, ethical, legal, clinical, demographic, and international aspects of the oral anovulants now commonly called "the pill." This analysis is important because over 25 million women now take these drugs and it is absorbing because the rapid popular adoption of this new technology is used by the author to examine some fundamental issues which influence the American way of life.

We should all share a grave concern for the giddy spiraling population of many countries particularly in Asia; for the widening gap between rich and poor, nations and people; and for the related problems of world hunger and malnutrition. The development of new contraceptive methods and the changing attitudes to sterilization and abortion have been hailed by many, perhaps a little prematurely, as answers to these problems. In my view, raised incomes, improved health, better diets for the poor, and a general increase in the quality of life are important catalysts to full acceptance of family planning in most societies, and of themselves should be the key goals of development. The advances in contraceptive techniques have allowed people to realize their own plans for desired family size and have provided women with the freedom to engage in sexual activities without the fear of pregnancy. The oral anovulants have contributed substantially to these important changes. But have we adequately measured the risks involved or the costs to society of adopting the wide use of these powerful drugs? While we have no doubt that the oral anovulants are almost unrivaled in their effectiveness in preventing pregnancy, do we have the evidence to declare unequivocally that they are safe under all conditions?

Birth control pills are not simple chemical compounds whose effects we understand or which are eliminated quickly from the body like many vitamins or commonly used medicines. The oral anovulants are powerful hormone pills containing usually both estrogens and progestogens. The complete action of these hormones is not known and their long term effects have never been investigated. The particular hormones used act on the pituitary gland. The pituitary, situated in the brain, is often termed the body's master gland because it controls many other hormone producing glands. A surgeon would rightly be extremely cautious when operating in the region of the pituitary because he knows that the slightest injury to that gland could cause death or result in a whole array of irreversible and bizarre symptoms. Yet there appears to be so much less concern in chemically tinkering with our hormone system including the pituitary.

FOREWORD

It must be acknowledged that all forms of medical treatment, including the simplest of drugs, carry some risk. But the question of risk with the pills deserves to be looked at somewhat differently because unlike other medicines they consist of a form of treatment given to a healthy, not a sick person, and to prevent a normal occurrence, not to treat an illness nor to immunize against a disease.

Unlike most other drugs, demand for the use of the anovulants is created by the mass media, by family planning campaigns, by changing attitudes towards sex, and as Dr. Merkin puts it by "our nation's propensity for the one best technological solution to a social problem." It is usually the patient who asks the doctor to prescribe the pill, whereas in most other instances the doctor persuades the patient of the necessity to take a medicine he is prescribing. This is an important distinction.

In the case of other drugs or treatments the physician must weigh the benefits against the risks. Therefore he will prescribe a drug known to be toxic if it is the only medicine which will influence the course of a serious disease like cancer or leukemia, whereas he would not take this risk for a mild self-limiting illness. But with "the pill" most doctors appear not adequately to have probed their consciences concerning risk. They have shrugged this off because the patient is demanding the drug and the regulatory agencies have approved its use.

What are the risks involved? As Dr. Merkin points out, there is no real answer to this question because the research has not been done. When presented with the available evidence doctors and scientists will provide very different interpretations of the same data presented to them concerning the pill.

We do know that the oral anovulants result in an increased risk of thrombo-embolic disease in which blood clotting in the vessels may lead to various symptoms, and sometimes to death. There is clear evidence that some women on the pill have an increased requirement for certain essential nutrients such as folic acid and vitamin B_6. A deficiency of folic acid is the second most common form of nutritional anemia (iron deficiency being the most prevalent). Recent studies indicate that oral anovulants alter carbohydrate metabolism in some women, the changes being characterized by impaired glucose tolerance and abnormally elevated serum insulin levels after oral glucose loads.

But what is really not known at all is the long term effects, if any, of taking such powerful hormone drugs. No group of women have yet reached the menopause, let alone old age, who began taking the pill in their late teens or early 20s. The first contraceptive pills only became available on prescription about fifteen years ago. All physicians involved should have a haunting fear that some unknown problem lies ahead for women who have taken the pill for many years and who began while quite young.

The dreadful story of diethyl-stilbestrol (DES) is strikingly told in this book. This compound related to those present in many anovulants, was for many years used to prevent miscarriages in pregnant women; it is the hormone our farmers have used to promote growth in the cattle and poultry we eat; and it is now gaining wide use as the morning-after contraceptive pill. It is known that DES was the cause of vaginal cancer arising in adolescent girls and young women some 15 or 20 years after their mothers had been prescribed DES during pregnancy to prevent miscarriage. Vaginal cancer is a most terrible disease. If diagnosed early it can be treated by mutilating surgery in a young person who has not fully realized the usefulness or pleasures of having a vagina; if neglected, the cancer spreads and leads to death.

But Dr. Merkin's book is not a catalog of evidence of the potential medical dangers of the pill. It puts these in perspective in order to furnish a setting for a balanced and critical analysis of the historical, social, legal, ethical, and societal factors related to the pill. But in a sense the oral anovulants which form the theme of the book, are skillfully used as a vehicle for examination of terribly important and basic human questions facing our society.

The book probes a system where physicians (and this is my profession) seem often to be more beholden to their professions than to their patients; where a greedy pharmaceutical industry maximizes profits while taking excessive risks with consumers; where a recalcitrant legal system is quite unable to reach consensus about who should pay the bill when something goes wrong; where an overworked and understaffed watchdog agency is unable to fulfill its responsibility to the American people; and where a wealthy class in the industrialized world remains quite unconcerned about its own poor citizens and is grossly negligent of its responsibilities to the developing countries.

At the end of the line we have citizens with no effective advocate and we have poor countries largely at the mercy of the industrialized nations and the giant multinational corporations. But public attitudes particularly in the U.S. and the Western world must also be blamed.

FOREWORD

We have developed a society which seeks to solve problems not by removal of their causes but by alleviating the symptoms, and as suggested in this book, by some new "technological fix." Thus, we attempt to deal with hunger in the U.S. by giving away food stamps, not by raising incomes or reducing deprivations which lead to poverty; we find heroin addicts and we substitute for that drug another one, methadone; we discover that per capita income is low so we counteract this with a birth control pill. As Dr. Merkin puts it, we are always looking for that "social aspirin."

My nine years of medical and nutrition work in East Africa, and my continuing involvement with several parts of Africa, Asia and Latin America, lead me to a special concern for those in the non-industrialized countries who are being encouraged to take the pill—and most of the urging has originated in the Western world. I am fully aware that some of these nations have serious population problems, and that large numbers of unplanned pregnancies and unwanted children do result in grave economic and other consequences for many families. But this is no excuse for our lack of concern about the dangers of technologies we transfer to these countries or for our neo-colonialist attitude toward the people there.

If the oral anovulants pose any threat to the nutritional status and health of American women who are in general overfed, and who have access to good medical facilities, then the risks to women in developing countries must be much greater. This is especially true because those most strongly urged to take the pill are often the poor and the deprived—and their deprivation includes the lack of an adequate diet and of good medical care.

Therefore, for example, the fact that oral anovulants can cause macrocytic anemia in the U.S. and U.K. must cause grave concern for those on the pill in countries like India where anemia due to folic acid deficiency is already known to be quite high in women of childbearing age. Yet practically no large scale monitoring of women taking the pill in family planning programs in developing countries has been reported.

Another area of serious concern to me is the possible effect of the oral anovulants, particularly those with a high estrogen content, in reducing the amount of breast milk produced in nursing mothers. In many poor countries if breast milk in sufficient quantities is not available, then the infant has little chance of survival, let alone of growing properly. Estrogens are used to suppress lactation in women who do not wish to breast feed their infants and who want their breasts to be quickly dried up after birth of a baby.

In developing countries many women are put on the pill fairly soon after delivery of an infant because this is a time when they are under medical care and it is thought to be a good psychological moment to decide not to have another child. Proper research is only now beginning to determine under field conditions the effects of the pill on lactation. The agencies pressing family planning in poor countries have been negligent in not adequately investigating this potential problem before now. There is also a potential risk to the infant of hormones from the pill which pass into the breast milk which is his food. It is not sufficiently appreciated that full lactation has a very definite effect on delaying ovulation. Breast feeding is very likely having a greater effect on reducing fertility in many countries than are all the artificial contraceptive methods combined. Yet we opt for the technological fix rather than for a simple, natural biologic method which carries with it great advantages for the child and some for the mother.

An interesting follow-up case study for Merkin or someone else to write would consist of an analysis of the spread of bottle feeding and the reduction in breast feeding. This is having disastrous consequences because bottle feeding frequently results in serious infantile diarrhea and the formulas are so expensive for poor families that they are often overdiluted and lead to malnutrition in the infant. Again the complex reasons for the shift to the new technology include profit-hungry and immoral sections of the food industry, a medical profession that has not shown adequate concern, and the spread of Western ideas (in this case concerning the human breast) which are inappropriate to many other societies.

In his conclusions Merkin goes further than I would in saying that he suspects that we already know enough about oral anovulants to justify removing them from the market. He believes that there is plenty of evidence of harm, and that despite their efficacy there are enough available alternatives with fewer risks.

But the main thrust of this readable and excellent book is that greater caution, candor, and concern for human life are needed. It is after all women's bodies which are being tampered with, and it is their lives which might be affected. This case study is not a blanket indictment of the pill; it is a humane examination of many important facets surrounding its use, and ones which apply to our society and our world

FOREWORD

in a very broad context. This book deserves a wide readership and it should have far reaching effects on public attitudes, on professional practices, and on government policy.

Michael C. Latham, M.D.
Professor of International Nutrition
Cornell University

PREGNANCY AS A DISEASE

1

INTRODUCTION

The real issue here is not drugs but subtle damage: the way societies come to grips with questions of therapeutic intervention. The traditional allopathic medical paradigm is criticized for disaggregating the human body for the sake of convenience.

We have all overheard examples of this ideology, which seeks to treat disease by counteracting the *symptoms* of the disease. One doctor to another: "I had a perforated uterus today – how did your day go?" Reply: "That bleeding ulcer kept me busy all morning." No mention is made of the human being attached to these pathologies, and we can be sure that such small talk suggests the nature of patient management implied by this medical shorthand.

Modern medicine, whether dealing with the uterus, the stomach, or a pregnancy, views its "facts" from a special perspective not necessarily synonymous with that of its clients — economists, sociologists, psychologists, lawyers, or theologians. I shall examine this special bias, arguing that the very interventions made by our physicians and pharmacologists too often result in social repercussions that may be considered "toxic" in themselves. The seeming immediacy of relieving pain, discomfort, or unwanted fertility results in reflexive, disjointed, and shortsighted measures that fail to consider the long-term consequences essential for optimum viability of the society. Means become confused with ends, as suggested by the medical quip, "The patient died in perfect electrolytic balance." One can readily imagine each specialist methodically practicing precisely what he or she has been trained to do under the circumstances, disregarding the socio-cultural context within which the "problem" originated. Or, "The operation was a success, but the patient died." Supportive evidence for the above position is too abundant: witness the fact that the mortality rate from cancer of the breast in women has not significantly improved over the past several decades, despite mass screening campaigns and new modes of therapy. Why? Probably in part because the objective is not simply to encourage women to come in for diagnosis, or to excise a malignant breast, but ultimately to prolong the effective lives of these women by detecting the cancer at an earlier stage (i.e., before the tumor has metastasized), and preferably, to prevent the cancer altogether. We may ask: Does Alka-Seltzer control or eliminate gluttony? Do tranquilizers reduce the stress of social disorganization, noise pollution, unemployment, or discouragement? Does methadone reduce drug habituation? Do birth control pills (hereafter referred to as "oral anovulants") put more food on the table and reduce poverty? In the short run, perhaps we can answer yes. In the long run, the answer is almost certainly an unqualified no. Who makes the judgment and what is our "proper" time frame? Traditionally, our physicians make the decisions, and the time frame is based upon the increasingly obsolete acute doctor-patient relationship premised upon immediate results.

I contend that when such myopic logic is extended to *social* pathology, the synergisms and amplifications of what outwardly appear to be localized interventions produce a surfeit of unanticipated consequences. This is not to say that the individual is forsaken.

Pregnancy as a Disease

Since most significant modes of contraception are placed under the jurisdiction of physicians, it follows that physicians' definitions of the situation are likely to be delimited by their conceptions of therapeutic intervention. Against what do physicians intervene? Against germs, malfunctioning organs, morphological deformities, deviant behavior, contagion, and disturbed homeostasis. These persons are trained and educated as biological scientists. When ovulation, menstruation, and conception are *defined* as pathological, is it not likely that the same mechanisms and theories that underlie the prevention of and therapy for dread disease are mobilized against the threat of pregnancy (and thus, against women)? Since medical intervention is supported and reinforced by legal and regulatory institutions like the courts and the Food and Drug Administration, their approach is legitimized and only the immediate effects and objectives are considered germane. Is there a health payoff for women who place themselves in the hands of their trusted physicians? Or does the simple fact that pregnancy — like a malignant tumor — is averted speak for itself? The oral anovulants, like the antibiotics, *work*, and epitomize what modern man is able to effect with sophisticated technology. Is their effectiveness sufficient? What else do these drugs do? We have succeeded in finding a social aspirin to alleviate social distress — i.e., population pressure. Yet even aspirin kills or causes anaphylactic reactions in some individuals each year (and has been linked with teratogenic effects in lower species in the offspring of mothers who ingested it during gestation). What about the risk of social toxicity in humans?

Social Toxicity

As suggested in the opening paragraph, the important question in this study concerns the nature of subtle damage. To understand social toxicity, we must be able to answer such questions as: Effect on what? When does the effect manifest itself? Must the damage be observable? Must it be measurable? Do we run the risk of being alarmists — and therefore, denying mankind a badly needed technique — when we attempt to anticipate or discover negative externalities that our current scientific prowess fails to suggest? Whose interests take precedence — the woman's, those of the fetus, the newborn, or the greater society? So much depends upon our time frame. For example, we know that oral anovulants somewhat reduce the quantity of breast milk in a lactating mother. We know that the hormones in oral anovulants cross the placental barrier (as do drugs that were widely used during pregnancy until the 1960s) and enter the fetus. What effects do these known phenomena have in terms of fetal, infant, and longer-term mortality and morbidity? Perhaps they take years to show up, in ways to which we are presently insensitive. Such effects would be an example of social toxicity.

What are the effects of a medical paradigm that gives control over one's body to the "experts," thereby depriving the individual of self-determination and self-expression in as crucial an area of being as health, life, and death? This could lead to a belief in the essentiality of external control (as in the example of drug dependency). Would it not be better to move in the direction of greater self-determination and independence?

The fact remains that we do not know the mechanism of action nor the long-term effects of many medicines that we use today; we would do well to refrain from using drugs unless we are quite sure that we are doing the individual minimal harm in relation to the expected benefit. This can be summed up in a quote from Dr. Mirkin at the University of Minnesota: "When drugs pass through the placenta, where do they go?" (Solomon, 1973). Perhaps even a generation's time is insufficient to tell us the answer.

Purpose

The purpose of this study is to link the traditional allopathic medical paradigm, which defines pregnancy as a disease, with the vital question of social toxicity as an iatrogenic effect. That is, does the definition of pregnancy as a disease result in what we may call "social diseases of treatment"? In an attempt to answer this question, we will examine the role technology plays in setting therapeutic alternatives, and the support our legal and regulatory agencies provide in assuring accountability and ethical behavior on the part of our trusted professionals. Oral anovulants will be used as a case study, since they are special in their impact, history, use, and probable long-term effects. The question remains: Are the real or potential negative externalities of interventions of this magnitude justified by the urgency and reality of rapid population growth? Or do the iatrogenic effects of oral anovulants outweigh — for the individual and the society — the risks associated with their use, given that technological and social alternatives exist?

2

PREGNANCY
AS A DISEASE

Modern contraception is generally equated with the sanctioning in June, 1960 by the United States Food and Drug Administration (FDA) of the synthetic oral anovulants* for contraceptive use. Thus, by legal and regulatory fiat, the era of chemical-dependent contraception began, and its evolution to date has typified what Wilkinson (Ellul, 1964: vi) characterized as the progressive technologization of our civilization — "the quest for continually improved means to carelessly examined ends." The Technological Man, a product of such civilization:

is fascinated by results, by the immediate consequences of setting *standardized* devices into motion. . . . Above all, he is committed to the never-ending search for *"the one best way"* to achieve any designated objective. [Emphasis added.]

At issue here is not the desirability of technological innovation, but the plausibility of the social, legal, and regulatory mechanisms required by the immensity and pervasiveness of these developments.

---

*The term "oral anovulants" is synonymous with "oral steroids," "oral contraceptives," or as they have become popularized, "the pill." Use of the term "the pill" can be misleading in that it suggests "that one brand has the same reaction on a woman as any other brand" (Okrent, 1971: 1). There is, in fact, considerable diversity in the type of "pill" marketed today: some are dominant in estrogens, others in progestins, and others evenly balance. Thus, "the pill" is an unfortunate euphemism for this class of synthetic pharmaceuticals which are marketed by several companies, and best prescribed with due regard for the great dif-

PREGNANCY AS A DISEASE

The underlying theme of inquiry asks: Do new forms of technological settings facilitate or impede social change, and under what conditions?

Morton Mintz (1970: 116) quotes Dickinson W. Richards, a 1965 Nobel Laureate in Medicine:

How far should we go, or try to go, in compounding drugs for our society? This suggests an allied and somewhat broader question: are we trying to work with nature or are we trying to work against and control it?

In the world at large, with all the vast technologies and powers now available, it would appear that man is moving along rather complacently in the belief that he will one day conquer nature and bring all its forces under his control. Perhaps he will. On the other hand, there is evidence that he is not controlling nature at all but only distorting it. . . . His powers have extended so far that nature itself, formerly largely protective, at least in the long and historical view, seems to have become largely retaliatory. Let man make the smallest blunder in his far-reaching and complex physical and physiological reconstructions, and nature, striking from some unforeseen direction, exacts a massive retribution.

Recent advances in biomedical technology, of which oral anovulants are a prime example, are certainly characterized by their instrumental complexity. But more important, these "advances" are often irreversible in their effects and devoid of agents who can be held accountable when something goes awry. Yet, when an infant is born with phocomelia (deformities of the upper limbs) because her mother took thalidomide as a sedative during her pregnancy, responsibility must be placed. The question remains—on whom? On the prescribing physician? On the pharmaceutical manufacturer? On the unsuspecting mother? On all three parties? Similarly, when genes are manipulated and result in teratogenic effects, there is no "going home again" — once and for all, a malformed human being has been created. And when the twelve-year-old daughter of a woman who ingested diethylstilbestrol

---

ferences in the "hormonal profiles" of the target women. (The Population Council states that by early 1969, twenty brands of oral anovulants were distributed in the United States, at a rate of about 8.5 million cycles per month (1971: 6). For present purposes, "oral anovulants" will be used throughout, since they imply the drugs' basic mode of operation, i.e., the inhibition of ovulation. The fact that these synthetic hormones are not identical with the body's natural hormones is important, and will be discussed in detail in the section on pharmacologic properties.

[8]

(DES) to prevent a miscarriage during the 1940s develops cervical or vaginal cancer, perhaps as a consequence, it ought not be unreasonable to demand extreme caution and the most thorough, intensive laboratory and clinical research possible to reduce the uncertainty before further prescription is permitted.

When the population exposed to the risk of death or severe untoward effects from such "therapeutic" intervention numbers in the tens of millions (as it does with the oral anovulants), and the upper limit theoretically consists of a large proportion of the world's women of reproductive age, it is not moot query to inquire, as Lasagna does (1962a: 203), "Who, then, shall pay the bill?" While the scale of the potential social and medical problems dramatizes such issues, it does nothing to decry the significance of a tragedy suffered by even one woman. This much-neglected and unresolved conflict between the individual and society, "between men and man" – between aggregate statistics and a single human life – is crucial to our understanding of accountability, risk, ethics, and the considerable shortcomings of our socio-cultural system. These problems will be addressed at some length in later chapters.

It is neither valid nor just to beg the question of responsibility, as has been our tradition, by focusing blame on the *uses* of technique.

Ellul (1964: 96-97) cautions:

There is an attractive notion which would apparently resolve all technical problems: that it is not the technique that is wrong, *but the use men make of it.* Consequently, if the use is changed, there will no longer be any objection to the technique.

. . . a principal characteristic of technique . . . is its refusal to tolerate amoral judgements. It is absolutely independent of them and eliminates them from its domain. Technique never observes the distinction between moral and immoral use. It tends, on the contrary, to create a completely independent technical morality. [Emphasis added.]

If "technical problems" are to be prevented or corrected, it is not sufficient to alter the use of a drug from contraceptive applications to gynecologic therapy (or vice versa), as, for example, it is not sufficient to change nuclear weaponry into power sources. These are, essentially, ethical questions of *social responsibility,* or in Parsons' (1969: 327) words, "responsibility to promote or at least do no harm to the values and welfare of the societal system and the various classes of its members."

Perhaps the discussion so far provides a workable entrée to the structure and dynamics of the health and medical care system in which controversy over responsibility has permitted dubious policy and practice to go inadequately censored. It is becoming increasingly imperative that we explicate our values and codify precisely how far we, as a society, are willing to go toward the advancement of the public interest and the protection of the unsuspecting or otherwise powerless citizen. This question is more complicated than it may at first appear, for not only are the forces dedicated to maintaining the status quo formidable, but the political and economic ramifications are considerable.

A decision to use the most "modern" or the "latest" technology implies that a *choice* has been made from among alternatives; at one level, such as the woman's decision to use oral anovulants, this is apparent. The woman visits her physician, requests or is otherwise encouraged to "go on the pill," and leaves with a prescription that she can fill for about two or three dollars. But the social, legal, economic, and clinical processes that led to the availability of (and her request for!) the oral anovulants behind the pharmacist's counter are not equally clear. While we may be able to determine why the oral mode of contraception has been "chosen," discovering the history of how these drugs ultimately reached the marketplace is thought-provoking and provides an interesting commentary on the slovenliness of our own self-regard. To find out why a woman has chosen to use an oral anovulant (as opposed to another form of contraception, or none at all), we can elicit a response of generally satisfactory validity by asking her. On the other hand, to understand why oral anovulants exist and are legally available to the public, we must dig and infer, after the fact, how we got to where we are. Ellul (1964: 81-93) further suggests that:

what can be produced must be produced. . . . Technical automatism may not be judged or questioned; immediate use must be found for the most recent, efficient, and technical process.

The evolution of techniques then becomes exclusively causal; it loses all finality. This is what economists such as Alfred Sauvy mean when they say that "by a slow reversal . . . production is more and more determined by the wishes of individuals in their capacity as producers, than by their decisions as consumers." In reality, it is not the "wishes" of the "producers" which control, but the technical necessity of production which forces itself on the consumers. Anything and everything which technique is able to produce is produced and accepted by the consumer. The belief that the human producer is still master of production is a dangerous myth.

Can it be possible that oral anovulants exist and are as widely accepted as they have become simply because technology is able to produce them? Ellul's remarks are highly conjectural, and his depiction of Technological Man as a mere pawn subservient to some vague "technical necessity of production" is found wanting; but the obligation to suggest and reify a more satisfactory explanation falls upon us. In fact, Ellul may not be too far from the mark; Viederman (1973: 7) observes that, "In times of crisis there is also a natural tendency to try to identify a villain. Man's role is often seen in terms of its negative consequences." Viederman goes on to quote a poem written by two sixth graders in Kensington, Maryland. The last stanza is as follows:

> If we didn't have people
> We wouldn't have pollution
> Get rid of people
> That's the only solution.

Steinfels (1972: 6) concludes this point by observing, in the context of psycho-manipulative drugs (as opposed to oral anovulants):

How drugs work to produce their effects is sometimes not yet understood by the experts, almost always not understood by the user, and in any case invisible. This contrasts with education, in which, except for manipulative procedures which might be branded objectionable, the student has some idea of what is being done to him, and consequently can react selectively or appropriate the experience with a certain dignity and continuity.

I contend that many of our social problems, in whatever sphere of existence we choose to examine, are the result of such oversimplified views of the world and our environments that our propensity to use ad hoc (Bateson, 1972: 488-493) explanations and procedures have been glaring in their impropriety. We have tended to view man as a *mechanism*, an automaton (witness Stimulus-Response Theory), who is only capable of making ad hoc, snapshot, reflexive, and piecemeal responses in designing and controlling his settings.*

---

* A "setting" is what happens when "two or more people come together in new and sustained relationships to obtain stated objectives.

PREGNANCY AS A DISEASE

Sarason (1972) offers a unique conceptual model of reality by viewing any social system — or sub-system — as a congeries of settings, contending that conflict is to be expected at the interface of such settings because the societal mosaic lacks sharp edges that fit cleanly in place. He stresses that confusion results when man attempts to comprehend "chronologically mature settings . . . that (cannot be understood) in terms of the psychology of individuals" — largely because settings "(reflect) a fascinating amalgam of unexamined values and ideas." As a consequence, we frequently find ourselves "barking up the wrong tree." Sarason believes that the real problem stems from our inability or unwillingness to comprehend the *rules* that determine the outcome of a specified setting. *The rules of creation* underly the problem.

In suggesting that "The more things change, the more things remain the same," Sarason observes:

[T] he social context from which a new setting emerges, as well as the thinking of those who create new settings, reflects what seems "natural" in the society. And what seems natural is almost always a function of the culture to a degree that usually renders us incapable of recognizing wherein we are prisoners of the culture. Those who create new settings always want to do something new, usually unaware that they are armed with, and will subsequently be disarmed by, categories of thought which help produce the conditions the new setting hopes to remedy.

In a word, both "new" and continued settings are only facades; the main reason so many of us have difficulty in keeping up with changes in reality — and thus, gaining a foothold for purposes of understanding — is that reality has not changed all that much. What we actually witness are changes in the *settings of reality,* which lead to the misperception of accelerated change in reality itself. Sarason notes (1972: 5) that:

Currently, pollution and population growth are the problems providing the most dramatic forum for raising the question of what is and what should be the relationships among the technology, social organizations, societal problems, and basic values.

Sarason argues that values are the "first basic problem," but not the necessary and sufficient condition for the creation of new settings: "Beyond values the creation of settings involves . . . substantive knowledge, a historical stance, a realistic time perspective, and vehicles of criticism." Understanding the goal (of a setting) is only the first step on the road to comprehension, for rarely do those creating new settings give sufficient attention to "anticipating problems and consequences" (1972: 17-18):

Anticipating problems and consequences is not a pleasurable activity, if only because it confronts one with how hard and long one may have to work. . . .

Finally, Sarason emphasizes the importance of maintaining a "universe of alternatives," or a pool of variety (in the language of Modern Systems Theory), for "consensus about values does not instruct one in how to create settings consistent with these values, and that is why the creation of settings is such an important problem" (1972: 20). Basically, we can sum up Sarason's unusual perspective by exhorting ourselves and others not to concentrate on outward manifestations to the neglect of inner forces. This is precisely the perspective I shall attempt to provide in this case study of the setting of oral contraception during this part of the twentieth century. Our first step lies in recognizing that, as Steinfels (1972: 6) puts it, "[our] society is drug-hungry." In this vein, although Steinfels is concerned with psycho-manipulative drugs, he asks: "If Ritalin is good for an overactive child, would it be good for a hyper-kinetic country?" (1972: 5). Although we are faced once again with the problem of differing levels and units of analysis (as well as with a different class of drugs), we might ask ourselves, "If oral anovulants are good for a woman who wishes not to become pregnant, would they be good for a country that wishes to reduce its fertility?" Or the converse, "If oral anovulants are good for a country that wishes to reduce its fertility, would they be good for a woman who wishes not to become pregnant?"

Returning now to consideration of the modernity of a piece of technology (in this case, oral anovulants), how is the most "modern" or the "latest" piece of technology adjudged to be so? In general, I believe, such judgment is not based solely on chronological appearance in time, although the assumption is often made that older methods have been superseded. Is the "latest" the safest? The most effective? The most economical? The most popular? The most complex? More specifically, why are coitus-related methods of contraception considered antiquated when coitus-independent methods become available? Perhaps the alleged sophistication of modern contraceptive methods is more mythical than real: a woman using the diaphragm does not suffer the biochemically esoteric complications linked with her peers who use the oral anovulants. Nor does the male using the condom face any untoward physical, physiological, or psychological complications. And yet, oral anovulants are considered by many to have ushered in the ultimate in contraceptive modernity.

What is the appeal of a therapeutic mode that contradicts a basic tenet of medicine, "First, do no harm?" Or a second one, which we may describe in the words of Dr. Alan F. Guttmacher (Mintz, 1970: 116) who, in 1959 — one year before the FDA permitted the oral anovulants to be marketed in the United States — anguished over the fact that:

The steroid pills violate a general medical principal. It is deemed safer to affect a target organ, in this case the uterus, tubes, or ovaries, directly, rather than to tinker with that affect through another organ, particularly when that organ is as important and complex as the pituitary gland. This master gland produces more than a dozen other chemicals and hormones, each regulating a vital body process, such as thyroid activity, water metabolism, and body growth.

Perhaps one place to look for an answer is the perceived rewards on the part of the woman, the physician, the pharmaceutical companies, and for the society at large. For the woman, the reward is a cheap, aesthetic, almost 100 percent effective guarantee against unwanted pregnancy; for the physician, convenience; for the pharmaceutical industry, massive profits; and for society at large, assurance that the latest technology is being employed toward a currently fashionable objective — slowing the nation's growth rate.

Do the risks associated with oral anovulants warrant the investments? It has been said that every time a physician prescribes a drug (or a patient ingests a proprietary drug like aspirin), an experiment is being conducted. Each is making a *judgment* that the risks are in some manner outweighed by the expected benefits. Given the grave nature of the reservations regarding these powerful, synthetic hormones, is it necessary, desirable, or ethical for them to be distributed and their use encouraged, especially in impoverished areas and developing countries where even rudimentary health and medical care is essentially unavailable? What are the ethical and social implications of the widespread use of these drugs, given the nature of the rigor of clinical trials, the variability among women of different populations, and the degeneration or lack of standards to the point where, in some Latin American countries, a woman can simply walk into a pharmacy and purchase a bag of oral anovulants off the shelf without a prescription?

An examination of the legal and regulatory apparatus in support of the patient and the public interest suggests that current inadequacies must be redressed. This includes the common law, where personal injury cases are litigated; the watchdog power of the FDA; and the special fiduciary relationship existing between patient and physician. The ramifications of insufficient guarantees of safety extend well beyond the realm of ethical* drugs, and encompass the major institutions of our society wherein occur potentially harmful *experiments* requiring human capital. In other words, aside from possible metabolic, nutritional, and constitutional threats to a woman's well-being, *what else do these drugs do to our society* (and others who may fall under our influence)?

As a society, we appoint (e.g., the Secretary of Health, Education and Welfare) and license (e.g., our physicians) individuals expressly to deal with these problems because we lack expertise, and because the massiveness and complexity of present-day verified bodies of knowledge (such as medicine, law, and economics) demand full-time specialists. In so doing, we retain certain controls on the performance and initiatives of these agents to whom we *entrust* our lives and well-being. Thus, society's professionals are *accountable* to our citizenry for their performance in their respective professional roles. Parsons (1969: 325-360), discussing what he terms the "Professional Complex," or the three interdependent basic professional functions of research, teaching, and practice, notes:

a "professional" element must establish an appropriate pattern of relationship to a "lay" element — whether the latter consists of patients, clients, students, or research subjects, and the former of practitioners, professors, or investigators.

This "appropriate pattern of relationship" is institutionalized, as in the

---

* "Ethical" drugs are drugs available only by prescription from a licensed physician (e.g., oral anovulants); they are contrasted with over-the-counter or proprietary drugs available without prescription and which may be purchased directly by the consumer (e.g., aspirin).

example of the physician and his patient, whereby the patient or "client" is seen as a participant in his own therapy. This is considered a more apt concept "than providing legal consent to what would otherwise be assault and battery by the physician" (Freund, 1968: ix).

Parsons (1969: 327-329) contends that control over professional responsibility is exercised essentially through three mechanisms: 1) "the discipline of the market"; 2) "legal and moral sanctions"; and 3) "public authority." However, a fourth mechanism, ultimately the most important and the last recourse of the offended claimant, is that of trust, or fiduciary responsibility. When this last mechanism breaks down, real problems arise for the individual and society. These issues will be developed in some detail in later sections, although Parsons' contribution provides us with an excellent takeoff for the analysis to follow:

[The central theme is] to focus on the indispensability of fiduciary professional responsibility in insuring accountability in the ethical contexts that involve professional function in important degrees and, secondly, to give a rough frame of reference for characterizing the alternative, complementary, and supplementary mechanisms for the concrete cases where professional responsibility alone will not suffice.

The preceding introduction is intended to provide the necessary backdrop and part of the intellectual tradition that will be developed in the following chapters. This will consist of an intensive review and analysis of the social demographic, legal, clinical, and ethical aspects of oral anovulants, especially as this mode of "therapeutic intervention" bears on the interplay of systems of accountability, risk, and the ethics of experimentation with human subjects.

Each body of literature provides piecemeal, generally atheoretical data of variable reliability and validity. As far as can be ascertained, this is the first comprehensive attempt to integrate the admittedly controversial findings of the laboratory and the clinic with a contextual analysis of the setting of fiduciary responsibility, legal precedent, and ethical codification focusing on oral anovulants as a case study.

A thorough assessment of the organizational setting within which virtually life and death decisions are made by professionals, by "experts" entrusted with the responsibility of collective and individual well-being, is long overdue.

Let me be more precise. A system appears to have evolved that sanctions the conduct of physicians who may be more beholden to their profession than to their patients; of pharmaceutical manufacturers who maximize profits while taking excessive risks with the lives and physical integrity of the indirect consumers of their products (you and I); a recalcitrant legal system; and an overworked, understaffed watchdog agency, the FDA, which possesses too little authority in areas of the public interest where the contrary is required. In this system, citizens lack an effective advocate, often finding themselves at the mercy of, rather than in control of, their own health, their medical care, that of their spouses or loved ones, and in some cases, even their lives. They are often unable to make well-informed, self-interested decisions that would optimize their contentment and productivity in the face of real or imagined crises. Basic to this rationale is the role of the mass media, which heightens the sense of urgency and drama as burgeoning political, economic, ecological, and social demands condition important decisions, frequently made without requisite caution and foresight.

The oral anovulants offer an excellent research focus because they are without exception powerful synthetic hormones taken by millions of women, and unique in two senses. First, according to Moore (1969: 507):

[The oral anovulants are] a treatment given to a healthy person to prevent a normal occurrence, rather than inoculation given to prevent fatal epidemic disease or a drug [or operation] employed to treat human illness.

Secondly, oral anovulants are unlike any other ethical drug in that demand for their use is created, not by the physician's prescription pad, but by the mass media, family planning campaigns, changing attitudes toward extramarital and premarital sex, and our nation's propensity to seek the one best technological solution to a social problem (e.g., rapid population growth). This is the framework for the setting.

The forums for the above-mentioned debates have ranged from the halls of Congress to the pages of the *Ladies' Home Journal,* and the problems argued have run the gamut from prescription of these compounds to sexually undeveloped youngsters to thromboembolic disease and cancer. The major issues remain unresolved, with acknowledged experts examining the same empirical data and arriving at polar interpretations regarding safety, dosage, policy, and the ethics of prescribing these drugs for any reason whatsoever. While these synthetic hormones are implicated in a variety of social, demographic, and political spin-offs, questions of control and regulation are tossed back and forth like a "hot potato" between the judiciary and the regulatory agencies, with no single professional discipline apparently willing to make a definitive commitment to well-designed and controlled testing, monitoring, and adjudication of these extremely popular and potent drugs.

The question remains: When pregnancy is defined as a disease, how does this mobilize (or immobilize) the medical profession, the courts, and the Federal government in terms of experimental safeguards, systems of accountability, the assessment of risk/benefit ratios, and *the acceptability of alternative methods of contraception?* Regardless of the value placed on avoiding pregnancy, is it not conceivable that the technology of modern medicine, as well as the socio-cultural supports underlying it, can by design or chance be mobilized against the very individuals and the society allegedly the targets for assistance? What may be permissible in the battle against an epidemic or a chronic degenerative disease may become acceptable in the "battle" against pregnancy; and this is not meant to sanction the theory and methods employed in the fight against diseases such as those alluded to above. Rather, these questions are equally applicable in numerous settings outside the realm of oral contraception in which the reader is particularly interested: e.g., the dissolution of the family, the failure of an educational institution, erosion of government, or organization for revolution.

Of the currently available means of contraception, oral anovulants are the most problematic because of their potency, complexity, mode of operation, and the fact that they represent a shotgun approach to "therapeutics"—rather than having a clean, direct effect on a target organ, they manipulate haphazardly a gland controlling several other major bodily functions. We argue that this type of ad hoc approach frequently leads to consequences unanticipated, uncontrollable, or irreversible.

We know that an increasing number of women are taking oral anovulants (Westoff and Westoff, 1971), and we know that new side effects and contraindications continue to be discovered. Can we, in light of this, continue to *assume* that our physicians, pharmaceutical manufacturers, courts, and regulatory agencies are keeping current, taking thorough patient histories, fitting prescriptions (for whatever mode) to each individual's unique circumstances, monitoring product quality, and pressing litigation when standards are violated? We cannot afford to assume anything of the sort.

Somewhere along the line, somebody has determined what is a "tolerable intrusion" on the health and well-being of virtually millions of women of reproductive age. What social problem is so urgent that caution may be thrown to the wind by "experts" who ideally pursue science with a healthy conservatism and abiding regard for the public welfare? What vested interests operate to obscure, deflect and deny evidence that oral anovulants are dangerous, despite their effectiveness — repeatedly disregarding admonitions for prospective epidemiological studies necessary to insure against harmful or fatal consequences of these drugs? How is the unsuspecting public to be reached and educated about the risk they are taking? Who is to determine the acceptable level of risk, or ought the concept of risk be qualified in favor of an approach that would allow no one to die or be permanently disabled as a result of oral anovulants? This topic will be examined in light of torts law which, for example, often deems it legally acceptable to permit the production of a product, *knowing* in advance that an undefined number will die as a result (e.g., unmarked railroad grade crossings), since guaranteeing that nobody would be so harmed would be prohibitively expensive.

These issues create neither a "straw man" nor a blanket indictment of our institutions; rather, they comprise an argument that urges greater caution, candor, and concern for human life and society to a degree not presently manifest. For the consequences of our present course of action pertain not only to oral anovulants and their sequelae, but also overlap many other aspects of modern post-industrial technological innovation (and intervention) such as transplantation, genetic screening, and amniocentesis.

Controversy is the keynote here — controversy over laboratory and clinical findings, the role of the courts and the FDA, professional accountability, safety of these drugs, and the social demographic impact of this contraceptive method. But with dialectic of this nature, synthesis must ultimately occur, and perhaps the time is ripe, once we have the facts and indicators laid out before us, for a more just and rational, and less haphazard, policy toward demographic target populations and, especially, the myriad women whose bodies are being tinkered with in a less than humane manner.

PREGNANCY AS A DISEASE

A review of literature suggests that many tentative statements can be made at this time regarding the safety of oral anovulants, and it is hoped that this investigation will contribute by clarifying the role of these drugs in furthering the public interest and the individual's right to contentment and freedom from premature death.

3

THE SETTING OF "THERAPEUTIC" INTERVENTION: DRUGS IN AMERICAN SOCIETY

The Pharmaceutical Mode of Therapy

A basic question each physician must ask, and one about which we, as sociologists, no doubt are curious, is that put forth by Dowd et al. (1971:4):

[How does one] determine whether a procedure should be considered experimental or therapeutic? Is the possibility of success the touchstone? Does *any* possibility of success indicate that a procedure is therapeutic? . . . If there is consent; should there be any distinction made between "therapeutic" and "experimental" procedures? Are there any significant differences between procedures which are potentially lethal and those which may affect the body in some other fashion?

Blumgart (*Daedalus*, 1969: 253) contends that:

Every time a physician administers a drug to a patient, he is in a sense performing an experiment. It is done, however, with *therapeutic intent* and within the doctor-patient relationship since it involves a judgement that the expected benefit outweighs the risk. . . . We can standardize drugs, but we cannot standardize patients; medical care of the patient demands adjusting the drug to the individual's unique characteristics. [Emphasis added.]

PREGNANCY AS A DISEASE

Blumgart continues (p. 254):

In the clinical management of the patient entrusted to his care, the physician must be certain that the expected benefit of a particular procedure outweighs the estimated risk.

In an excellent and lucidly written volume edited by Paul Talalay, *Drugs in Our Society* (1964), Owsei Temkin traces the historical basis for drug therapy back to several thousand years B.C. He notes (p. 3):

To say that a drug has magic associations means that its action for good or bad does not depend on its natural qualities alone. The favor of a god, the observance of ceremonies, the absence of demoniac enemies, the healing *intent* of the dispenser — any or all of these factors are needed to make it therapeutically effective. [Emphasis added.]

How far can we be said to have progressed from this, the philosophy of the Sumerians, the Egyptians, or the Greeks? Are we any closer to a more accurate *knowledge* of experimentation or therapy — or can we say that little but the settings have changed?

Historical Initiatives

If we consider the writings of the Greek physicians from the Hippocratic era around 400 B.C., and ending with the work of Galen, we find that an attempt was made to "establish a physiological explanation of drug action." It became the physician's duty to recognize the nature of the disease in the individual and to treat the pathology with methods appropriate to the individual, taking into account such considerations as age, constitution, and even the season of the year. In other words, not only was the diagnosis specifically fitted to the physician's knowledge of his patient, but the therapy was to be individualized, as well (Temkin: p. 4). Temkin continues:

The Galenic physician in the Middle Ages and Renaissance believed himself in possession of a science of pharmaco-dynamics which was to help him in selecting the right drugs in right proportions for the treatment of his individual patient. The drugs were *tools* which the learned physician alone could use, if and when necessary. This distinguished him from the apothecary, who knew the drugs but not man, and from

the empiric, who at best had learned by experience of some remedies efficacious against certain symptoms or disease entities. [Em-
phasis added.]

While the movement from magic to naturalism gave the appearance of a new rationality, this was more implied than real, for while
natural causation had the outward signs of true empiricism, it nevertheless allowed for a certain amount of magic in its armamentarium.

Much as the Galenic system stressed the physiological basis of drug
action, it admitted a class of drugs that were effective in certain cases,
although nobody could say why. (Temkin: p. 4)

This gap permitted quacks to flourish, and in response the physician
bolstered his professionalism and reputation by the acquisition of an
academic degree " and the reliance on remedies that had been used for
centuries. . . ."

But Galenic physicians were soon challenged by the followers of
Paracelsus, who stressed the internal use of drugs chemically prepared
from substances often considered to be toxic. The uniqueness of the
Paracelsists stemmed from their abandonment of the tradiitonal phar-
macopoeia that underlay Galenic medicine, and the conflict was not
fully resolved until the Galenists disappeared and the Paracelsists were
depleted around the beginning of the eighteenth century. Both groups,
apparently, had become victims of the scientific revolution of the
seventeenth century. By this time, chemical drugs were firmly im-
planted in the physician's therapeutic rationale, and the apothecary
who prepared them in his laboratory became a chemist of note during
the eighteenth century. This is not meant to imply that medicine had
stabilized and routinized any particular doctrine following the dissolution of the Galenist and Paracelsist therapeutics; quite the contrary.
Temkin observes (p. 5), "If one wants to characterize the situation
around 1850, 'chaotic' is probably the most appropriate term." Furthermore, by about the early 1830s, an unusual proportion of practicing
physicians elected to abandon the "art of healing to devote themselves
full time to subjects which did not bring them into contact with patients." This phenomenon was unusual for two reasons: on the one
hand, these were men who had studied medicine, who held medical
degrees, were typically licensed to practice medicine, were members of

medical school faculties, and who were not pursuing or interested in healing. On the other hand, this marked the start of a revolution in the history of medicine, for these men "claimed knowledge had to be gathered before healing could hold promise." These were pragmatic reformers, who either by design or coincidence, decided to regroup and seek knowledge before engaging any further in its application (Temkin: p. 10).

During this lull in practice, the science of pharmacology emerged as part of physiology; responding to the needs of the therapist, it sought answers in the laboratory, and then turned this knowledge over to the practitioner.

On the one hand its task was to establish the active substances within the drugs, to find the chemical properties responsible for the action and prepare synthetically drugs that were more effective. On the other hand, it had to study the changes brought about by the drug in the organism and then explore the possible influence of such changes upon pathological conditions. (Temkin: p. 11)

Without going any more deeply into the strides that were being made in medicine and pharmacology during this important period in the history of science, I would like to address two concluding points. The period around 1876 marked the emergence of what was to become the pharmaceutical industry that we know today; there was no alternative, no turning back. While the pharmaceutical industry was only in the embryonic stage, it is fascinating to observe that even at this time, complaints began to be sounded that today have a familiar ring. Temkin (p. 12) quotes Buchheim, who lamented during this period:

The chemical industry of our days produces various substances for which no market can as yet be found. Under these circumstances, the idea suggests itself that it might be possible to use these products as drugs. We know a great number of physicians, without rhyme or reason, go after every new remedy that is recommended to them. *If an industrialist is but shrewd enough to advertise sufficiently, he usually succeeds in increasing the sale of his product* — for some time at least — and thus enriching himself. [Emphasis added.]

Temkin concludes his piece on a philosophical note, observing that in spite of our interest in and enthusiasm for the history underlying the development of what is today the sophisticated "science" of medical pharmacology, we must realize that some things (reality?) have not changed.

In short, there is still the history of the attitudes toward drug therapy. And this is the history of human beings perhaps not wiser but hardly more foolish than we are. And it is the history of times and circumstances which they shaped or to which they responded just as we do today. (p. 13)

Techno-Scientific Innovation

Gaddum (Talalay, 1964: 17-26) provides us with additional insights into the development of the interaction between technology and science, focusing primarily on the information available from pharmacologic studies. This Gaddum breaks down into: 1) mode of action; 2) absorption and fate; 3) potency; and 4) toxicity and side actions. Noting that all of the aforementioned can be studied in both animals and humans, Gaddum goes into some detail about the meaning of each important aspect of pharmacologic research. I shall comment briefly on a few of the more relevant points. First, Gaddum (p. 23) contends that:

it is possible to reduce the risk that new drugs will produce unexpected effects when they are first put on the market, but it is probably impossible to eliminate it completely. It is, therefore, very important that there should be an effective organization for collecting as rapidly as possible all information about toxic effects on man which might be due to treatment. In the past, the arrangements for collecting this clinical information have been inadequate, but various bodies have been discussing this problem during the last year or two, for it is the most important part of our defenses against the adverse effects of new drugs.

Individual manufacturers have their own schemes for collecting information on drug reactions, but there is a feeling that something more should be done on a national or international scale.

Second, Gaddum notes the existence of two opposing forces – a dilemma, actually, whereby ". . . official regulations designed to make new drugs safe will stop the advance of therapeutics." (It has been suggested that if penicillin were to be discovered today in the United States, the stringency of FDA pretesting procedures would not permit it to be marketed for another ten years.) On the other hand, the danger of over-population results when disease is eliminated. Gaddum contends that medical science has enabled humans to tip the balance of nature, although through improvements in agricultural technology, the "intelligent use of birth control," and the planning of old folks' homes and hospitals, these side effects of modern medicine — longer lives and the survival of the otherwise unfit — can be mitigated.

Gaddum's contribution to our understanding is derived from the following observation (Talalay, 1964: 24-25):

The bad effects of drugs must be balanced against their good effects. Most drugs, including alcohol and aspirin and penicillin, have toxic effects and cause deaths every year, but no one proposes to prohibit their use, because their good effects are believed to outweigh their bad effects. . . . A new drug cannot be condemned just because it is found to cause occasional toxic effects; it is sometimes necessary to know how often these toxic effects occur among those exposed to the drug and also how much good the drug does, so that bad effects may be weighed against the good effects. It is usually very difficult to get quantitative information of this kind.

And yet, although cognizant of the above, we would be remiss in failing to concede the possibility that *any* intervention is precisely that — an imposition of considerable complexity on the natural order. Dickinson W. Richards (Talalay, 1964: 34-35) stresses that we must hold the fundamental order of nature in all due deference and acknowledge "both the concept and the evidence of teleology or design; [he believes] that one can profoundly dislocate this order only at great peril. It would seem better to try to discover this design rather than to override it."

Richards considers the perspective of René Dubos who, in writing "Medical Utopias," suggests "that the objective of society ought properly to be [a movement] toward fewer and fewer drugs rather than more and more, and fewer doctors also, for that matter, until it can get along with none" (p. 27).

Now this is admittedly an ideal situation, especially given the nature of Dubos' arguments in his work, *Mirage of Health*, although the underlying rationale is well worth considering. Although Dubos' utopia might be desirable, it is unlikely that it will come to pass or be popularly accepted as a societal objective for many years to come. We are already too much committed to a view that leads to more drugs and more physicians — our traditions and philosophies of the past few thousand years have a certain momentum of their own. An alternative utopian conception, offering a drug for every behavior and need and a high ratio of physicians per unit of population, is far more likely to be approximated Dubos argues (Talalay, 1964: 37):

In practice, the discovery of most new drugs has come from the primitive but nonetheless useful faith that for each biological [and shall we ask, social] threat, there exists in nature [society?] some substance capable of counteracting the action of this threat.

Continuing, Dubos (pp. 38-39) notes:

Most of the biological, physiological, and biochemical research has been focused on the study of the phenomena *which are common to all living things* [e.g., reproduction]. From the point of view of scientific philosophy, the largest achievement of modern biochemistry has been the demonstration of the fundamental *unity* of the chemical processes associated with life. . . .

While this so-called fundamental approach has been universally fruitful for the discovery of the structures and reactions which are *common* to all forms of life, it has almost completely failed to provide information concerning the structures and reactions which determine the *peculiarities* of each organ and function. As a result, the search for metabolic inhibitors [or ovulatory inhibitors] has been limited to attempts at interfering with processes ubiquitous in all living things, *for the simple reason that these are the only ones which are known.* Powerful metabolic inhibitors have been synthesized on the basis of this knowledge, but in general *they lack selectivity* [recall our earlier discussion of "shotgun" therapeutics and the manipulation of a master gland, the pituitary, in the quest to prevent ovulation]. Being directed against fundamental processes, they affect many different biological functions [and heretofore not considered socio-cultural functions] and are therefore likely to exhibit various forms of toxicity [and, to coin a phrase, "social toxicity"] which sharply limit their usefulness. [Emphasis added.]

Drug Selectivity

Dubos' stance is that a truly rational approach to the discovery and prescription of drugs requires a fundamentally different type of knowledge from that currently in vogue in biological research. He believes that "not much progress can be made until there is a shift of emphasis from the phenomena characteristic in life *in general* to the particular reactions and structures which give to each organ and function its unique characteristics." Cannot we take the next step and aspire to a research and praxis which take into account "the particular reactions and structures" which give to each individual and culture its unique characteristics? This, I should think, is basic, given the current nature of biological and societal interventions, be they therapeutic or otherwise. But some will disagree.

Social Toxicity

The concept of selectivity alluded to briefly above is an important one, and deserves further consideration. Selectivity denotes the specificity with which an active substance interacts with another particular living or chemical substance — and that alone. Dubos (p. 41) informs us:

It can be taken for granted that a biologically active substance will have some form of toxicity if it is capable of reacting with structures or functions ubiquitous in the living world. . . . Selectivity . . . is never absolute.
Even a highly selective drug is therefore likely to react with some structure other than the one for which it has been designed. *In other words, absolute lack of toxicity is an impossibility, because absolute selectivity is a chemical impossibility.* [Emphasis added.]

As much as I would prefer to refrain from the use of absolutes as qualifiers, concurrence with the above statement leads one inextricably to the conclusion that, with oral anovulants, we must *always* expect adverse effects, though they may vary in type and degree. Even the most "perfected" oral anovulant is, at least theoretically, not immune from untoward side reactions in some segment of the population. This no doubt applies at many levels — from the biological through the societal. Recognizing this, perhaps by implication, Dubos (p. 41) continues:

Absolute lack of toxicity is a will-o'-the-wisp for another reason — namely, that any action on any particular structure or function of an organism bids fair to alter the integration of this organism as well as its relation to the environment. All forms of interference with organismic integration or with ecological relationships are likely to have in most cases indirect consequences, always difficult to predict and often potentially dangerous. In other words, even though a drug is not toxic per se, it may exert effects which are indirectly harmful to the organism.

Returning once again to the topic of psychotomimetic drugs (but with equal applicability to the oral anovulants), Steinfels (1972) prompts the following remarks from Dubos (p. 42):

The problems posed by the forms of toxicity which involve organismic integration will become of increasing importance as [these] drugs are more widely used. Such problems obviously transcend the orthodox science of toxicology. Their understanding will demand a sophisticated knowledge of what constitutes an integrated organism, above and beyond the properties of its isolated parts. [Amen]

But this concept of "social toxicity" is even more ephemeral than that of physical, biological, or ecological toxicity. This study aims to contribute to an understanding of the social setting within which these drugs are developed, promulgated, used, and often abandoned.

Earlier, I alluded to our tendency to use reductionistic (e.g., stimulus-response) explanations and models, "designed for the study of single variable systems, expressing themselves in rapidly developing effects." Likewise, most drug research has been of this type, focusing on simple cause-effect relationships. While this approach may be adequate for revealing the direct effect of drugs — be they useful or toxic — particularly within a short time following their administration, they fall far short of what is required for the more complex dimensions of drug research.

Dubos (p. 43) observes that:

practically all biologically active substances have a multiplicity of secondary effects, not readily predictable from the observation of simple cause-effect relationships. Furthermore, these indirect secondary effects often unfold slowly, as the living system under consideration (ranging from an organ system to a socio-cultural system) progressively develops, differentiates, undergoes adaptive modifications, or simply becomes older.

Long-Range Effects

One of the most controversial points about oral anovulatory drugs is their long-range effects on the person using them (and, of course, the society at large). Dubos' (pp. 43-44) insights are particularly astute on this point, as well:

The study of the toxic effects of drug treatment therefore requires long-range observations made from two different points of view. On the one hand, it must concern itself with primary and secondary effects far removed in time from the moment of administration of the drug under consideration. On the other hand, it must bring to light secondary effects very different in mechanism from those corresponding to the initial impact of the drug and affecting sites and characteristics of the treated animal or man other than those primarily affected.

To a very large extent, the study of the long-range effects of drugs has been limited so far to the statistical analysis of observations made on large populations. However, the results of such analyses are often unconvincing; witness the controversies created by the use of anticoagulants or anovulatory drugs.

Clearly, a more inclusive, integrated, and multi-factorial model of man is needed, particularly in this critical area of drug research.

Drug Efficacy

Goodman (Talalay, 1964) contributes to our emerging scenario of techno-scientific intervention by detailing the semantics of "drug efficacy." But I shall not belabor the point regarding conceptual and methodological problems inherent in demonstrating drug effectiveness. The reader is referred to Goodman's piece for an interesting perspective on the subtleties involved. However, Goodman contributes to the clarification of some of the aforementioned networks through the development of a paradigm which he entitles, "ABC of Drug Efficacy," or the dynamics of the patient-physician-drug complex. The discussion disaggregates this triad according to some components of each factor, while at the same time overlooking a major fault of the paradigm: i.e., it is really not a triangle, but a square, with the missing corner perhaps being labeled "societal factors." But first, let us examine the paradigm in Goodman's original formulation. Emphasizing its basis in human (rather than animal) research, Goodman (pp. 52-53) constructs the following typology:

A. *Drug Factors*

Doses employed
Multiple effects
Absorption
Distribution
Metabolic rate
Excretion
Duration of effect
Route, duration of administration
Habituation
Addiction liability

Drug interactions
Tolerance
Side-effects
Toxicity
Idiosyncracy, hypersensitivity
Margin of safety
Precautions
Contraindications
Pharmaceutical properties
Chemical properties

B. *Patient Factors*

Sex, age
Body size, weight
Pregnancy
Pharmacogenic factors
Biochemical status
Nutritional status
Drug metabolism
Disease
Idiosyncracy, hypersensitivity

Cost
Contraindications, precautions
Toxicity
Margin of safety
Concomitant therapy
Personality factors
Attitudes toward disease,
        drugs, doctors
Halo and milieu influences

C. *Physician Factors*

Training
Diagnostic skill
Therapeutic skill
Experience with drugs
Concomitant therapy

Attitude toward drug therapy
Attitude toward patient
Attitude toward disease
Halo and milieu influences

I suggest we include the fourth factor, that involving society, in something such as the following format:

D. *Societal Factors*

Cultural influences
Family structure
Sex roles

Education/literacy
Language
Dietary habits

D. *Societal Factors (continued)*

Occupational structure	Normative structure
Socio-economic structure	Philosophy
Religious influences	World View

The reader will immediately perceive that the elements are not mutually exclusive, nor are they exhaustive. But it is likely that they are valid and representative of the multi-factorial network underlying the "ABC's" of drug efficacy. Even Goodman recognizes that "at best, [animal studies of] pharmacology provides only paradigms and analogies, the clinical predictive value of which remains to be demonstrated. The best model for a cat is another cat. The best model for man is man himself" (pp. 52-53). The best model for society is neither cat nor man, and that comment is not intended to be superfluous.

Goodman (pp. 53-54) calls attention to his intentional neglect of the *mechanism of action* of drugs since, he acknowledges, "there are very few drugs, if any, for which we know the basic mechanism of action. *Drug action is not drug effect. The effect results from the action of the drug.*" [Emphasis added.]

I think it is not overstating my argument to contend that there are *no* drugs for which we know the basic mechanism of action since, in truth, what we connote by mechanism of action is the setting of the effect — "Almost without exception, the investigator is merely describing an effect, and he has contributed nothing whatsoever to basic knowledge about drug action. Even when we think that the basic action has been elucidated, additional research nearly always indicates that the goal is still elusive" (p. 54). Here we have a prime example of the never-ending search for that ephemeral "nth" variable — best put, in the words of Goodman, by Horace Davenport. Known as the "law of the specificity of enzymes," this states "the specificity of an enzyme is inversely proportional to the length of time the enzyme has been around" (p. 57).

Drug factors are of special importance in that it is vital that we recognize the multiplicity of effects associated with any given drug. Goodman (p. 55) notes:

Every known drug exhibits multiple effects. The more intensively a drug is studied, the more new effects are discovered. Even in the dose given to obtain a particular desired result in animals or man, a variety of effects can be detected by the careful observer. This fact is glossed over and often forgotten, so that one repeatedly hears about *the* effect of a drug or, worse yet, the *specific* effect of a drug. . . . The *total* spectrum of responses to a drug enters into the efficacy picture. . . . The clinical usefulness and the safety, and hence the efficacy, of a drug may be sharply curtailed by the degree to which the desired therapeutic effect is bracketed by these extraneous effects.

Drug efficacy is a highly *relative* concept, one which we must more often take into account by asking, "Relative to what?" Goodman (p. 62) observes, "Indeed it is sometimes impossible to distinguish between therapeutic and toxic effects."

I wish to emphasize the difficulties inherent in disaggregating "social therapy" from "social toxicity," considering what we know about the difficulties alluded to above in the purely clinical setting. But, as has been so often said, "it is often difficult to see the forest through the trees," and that may be our major obstacle to knowledge in this area of drugs and society. We stand in the midst of the very setting which we hope to explicate. Such a stance has frequently led us to ask the wrong questions; as Lasagna (Talalay, 1964: 98-99) suggests, we have a history of choosing "irrelevant variables of response."

Thus, for example, one sees drugs which are planned for use in chronic diseases whose effects are only measured acutely. [Or] . . . focusing on temporary changes in measurable tumor size when one is really interested in the life span of cancer patients, or in the reduction of blood cholesterol when one is really interested in the prevention of deaths from coronary artery disease.

Or, one might add, focusing on the efficacy of preventing ovulation when one is really interested in lowering a population's growth rate — or prolonging and easing a woman's secure, contented, and healthy life. Lasagna (p. 103) concludes:

whatever deficiencies there may be in our evaluation of the therapeutic efficacy of compounds, these are small as compared to our ability to quantify the untoward effects of drugs . . . we cannot choose between drugs unless we know accurately what toxicologic price we must pay for their use.

Legitimation

Wintrobe (Talalay, 1964: 107) offers the weighty opinion that "the desire to take medicine is the greatest feature which distinguishes man from his fellow creatures." He points out that:

there are remedies for every complaint, and they are consumed in large quantities. Some members of our modern society behave as if life were a process of existence which can barely be maintained or endured without taking a continuous series of wonder drugs.

The pharmaceutical solution to living and societal well-being has been with us for millenia, and is likely to be with us long into the future. While adverse drug reactions have also been with us, no doubt for as long, "the attention given to adverse reactions is recent." Wintrobe continues (pp. 108-109):

There is a mistaken impression on the part of some who lately have become aroused about the problem of drug reactions that the testing of drugs in a sufficient number and variety of animals will provide the information which will call attention to adverse effects of drugs and will thereby protect prospective human recipients. While it may be true that in certain instances more adequate laboratory tests should have been carried out and in others clues concerning possible adverse effects were ignored for various reasons, nevertheless it must be recognized that laboratory tests cannot eliminate completely the risk involved in the taking of drugs.

Wintrobe continues (p. 110):

Heretofore, medical science has been satisfied with a haphazard approach. It has depended on the chance recognition of an untoward effect and, even more unpredictably, on the reporting in the medical literature of such adverse reactions, their ultimate recognition as such, and the eventual wide dissemination of this information to all persons concerned with the use of the drug in question.

The law is the recorded repository of society's willingness to act in defense or perpetuation of its norms, values, and interests.

The role of law in safeguarding the public trust, either through the imposition of sanctions or the redress of misconduct, is questioned here. Controversy exists about whether the courts are the proper place to resolve ethical issues relating to pharmaceutical manufacturing, sale, distribution, and use. (It has been suggested that such issues are in the domain of the regulatory agencies, such as the FDA.)

Toward resolution of these points, numerous legal scholars (Freund, 1969: 314; Calabresi, 1969: 387; Jaffe, 1969: 406; Cavers, 1969: 427) have addressed various facets of the role of law in legitimizing drug use and correcting injustices and liberties taken with the public interest. This literature will be reviewed and included in the research focus involving oral anovulants in Chapter 8.

It is especially interesting to examine how suits have been litigated between patient and physician, patient and pharmaceutical manufacturer, and among patient, physician, and pharmaceutical company. Of particular importance here, I believe, is that no separate body of law exists for the adjudication of these issues — plaintiffs must resort to the common law or torts law. Thus, we find the theory of strict liability, negligence, and breach of warranty* of critical value here.

Control

Fundamental to the issue of control is the question of whether the prevention of a normal occurrence (in this case, pregnancy or ovulation) is equivalent to the prevention and management of a disease. Can it logically be shown that:

$$\text{All therapy} \longrightarrow \text{All experiment}$$
$$\text{No therapy} \longrightarrow \text{No experiment}$$
$$\text{No experiment} \longrightarrow \text{No therapy}$$

All therapy, as has already been pointed out, is experimental, with a judgment being made by some party that the risk incurred by the therapeutic procedure is outweighed by the expected advantages. The question then becomes one of control over the process of therapeutic/technological intervention, for techniques of disease control are not functional equivalents, especially insofar as these techniques overlap social problems or otherwise "normal" occurrences.

---

*I wish to thank Harvey Yates, a friend and graduate of Cornell University Law School, who suggested the possible applicability of the theory of inverse condemnation, and who provided astute insight into the legal and regulatory aspects of oral anovulants.

Accountability

The issue of accountability overlaps the questions of control and legitimation. To whom are our legal, medical, and regulatory agencies accountable for the quality of their performance in their roles? What social mechanisms exist to insure the well-being of the individual and protect the public interest? How do the courts interact with the regulatory agencies, and how does private industry interact with professional associations? Where is the consumer — the client, if you will — amongst this complex network of power, authority, and reward? Who is looking out for him or her?

Accountability will be analyzed in light of Parsons' paradigm, as mentioned in Chapter 2. Various alternatives will be considered, and current approaches will be scrutinized.

4

SCOPE AND METHODS

An undertaking such as this, which attempts to synthesize existing research and exposition from disciplines as diverse as law and nutrition, necessarily precludes traditional methodologies and research designs.

Survey methods offer little but attitudinal orientations, information not at issue except as it has led to the *organization* of services within institutional settings. Attitudes of women who take oral anovulants have been plumbed, and may be useful in generating a demographic profile — but they are obviously insignificant when it comes to understanding the deficiencies of a social system in action. Furthermore, sufficient surveys of experts, practitioners and pharmaceutical manufacturers have been conducted so that replication would be redundant and superfluous for present purposes. In brief, we already *know* what the problems are.

Each discipline under consideration possesses its own peculiarities with respect to issues it considers vital, methods of generating and testing hypotheses, the routinization of its theory, and the embodiment of its setting in relation to other areas of knowledge. While we may sometimes appear to be comparing apples and oranges, in fact we must discover the systemic linkages that enable us to move, albeit hesitantly, among the components of our intellectual environment. Patterns can be discerned, and perhaps it will always be the case that policies will be formulated, with incomplete (and sometimes inaccurate) information. But where valid data exist, there is no excuse for not using them; as

Claude Bernard has written (Goodman, 1964: 51), "An hour of synthesis is worth years of analysis," and I contend that we in the social sciences are in the position of having rooms full of data untouched by human thought.

The disciplines considered relevant here will be discussed and integrated on the following pages. The reader will observe that the argument is totally dependent upon secondary data sources.

Social Demography and Technological Innovation

Social demography is a relatively new field concerned with the reciprocal relationships between sociological variables, such as social organization, and the elemental demographic variables of fertility, mortality, and migration (Ford and De Jong, 1970; Davis, 1964; Hauser and Duncan, 1969).

Broad in scope and interdisciplinary by definition, social demography provides an appropriate context within which to examine the setting of the social institutions charged with the health and well-being of society. At another level, social demography offers frameworks capable of quantitatively and qualitatively depicting populations accepting and exposed to the risk of complications resulting from various contraceptive techniques.

While abundant literature exists describing "acceptor" characteristics, contrasting the relative popularity and efficacy of different contraceptive modes, and increasing the diffusion of these innovations, the lack of literature assessing the safety and societal impact of oral anovulants is conspicuous. Considerable research is devoted to effectiveness, cost-benefit analysis of alternative methods of contraception, overcoming cultural and motivational obstacles to family planning, and the development of educational and mass media campaigns geared primarily to low-income populations in the United States and abroad; little research and education are directed toward informing the public of the concomitant risks associated with oral anovulants. Why?

Is it not incumbent upon the physician, the journalist, the family planning program administrator, the population policy maker, to share the ethical responsibility in the event that individual or collective trust is violated, when safety is not given its due regard? In addition to determining how best to reach a socially valued objective (such as limiting a population's growth rate), it is only fitting that the broader social implications of the techniques themselves be judiciously scrutinized. On the one hand, we have often asked, "How do we encourage a population to reduce its fertility by using the latest piece of technology, such as the oral anovulants?" On the other hand, we have been remiss in not asking of our authorities and ourselves how we can justify the use of a technique that may cause irreversible changes in a woman's body. When untoward effects occur, can no one be held accountable, when we already possess techniques that are simple, direct, reversible, and if used properly, give very considerable protection against unwanted pregnancy?

Oral Anovulants as a Case Study

This literature will be surveyed with an eye to the extent of use of oral anovulants both in the United States and abroad, together with the proportionate amount of attention devoted to safety, regulation, and related issues of mass experimentation and the long-range impact of technological innovation. Of special interest will be the use of oral anovulants in developing countries where, one can safely say, many target women suffer from medical and nutritional disorders that are likely to be complicated by the ingestion of synthetic steroids without adequate examination, follow-up, or supervision. Tragically, these same countries are those with the highest population growth rates, the least equitable distribution of wealth, and a readiness to accept a quick, inexpensive, modern "technological fix" popularized in the post-industrial countries. Furthermore, it is not fortuitous that these same populations, especially in the Caribbean and in Latin America, have served as guinea pigs for initial clinical trials of these drugs before they were permitted to be marketed in Rochester, New York or Butte, Montana. Who is to protect the vulnerable? Adams (1973: 842), for example, comments on the "selection of institutionalized patients as research subjects," but her remarks are equally applicable to the impoverished populations of developing countries:

[The deprivation of social opportunity] . . . makes them a particularly vulnerable, easily accessible, captive group, a hazard they share with prisoners, who belong to basically dehumanizing systems where social isolation and the pervasive undermining of human rights and dignity make it hard to exercise unbiased options about co-operating in establishment-supported projects.

It is worth pondering that Enovid, the first oral anovulant marketed in the United States, was first tested in Puerto Rico. Approximately five or more deaths occurred in the research population — all who died were relatively young women in their reproductive years — and curiously, no autopsies were performed. The official cause of death was listed as cardio-vascular incident — quite possibly a euphemism for thromboembolic disease. But it seems that we shall never know with certainty. One cannot help but wonder why.

The use of oral anovulants has been described as the largest experiment ever conducted on a group of otherwise normal, healthy women of reproductive age (it is estimated that at any given time, *20–50 million* women take these drugs world-wide).

Perhaps we can summarize the important questions as follows:

1.   Who should have the authority to decide whether a woman is given a medication that has a known or estimated risk of death or disability associated with it; that would, if used "properly," protect against pregnancy; that also has a known, estimated risk of death or disability?

2.   If users are given adequate education, warning, and information regarding risk, without medical supervision and approval, is the availability of technological innovation not better than the alternatives? (Recall that alternatives are not functional equivalents.)

3.   Is the rigidity of the medical profession due to its legitimate concern with the woman's well-being (given the alleged sloppiness of many physical examinations and prescriptions), or more to a concern with profit and control by forcing women to visit periodically for new prescriptions and physical examinations? (Although laws, regulations and practice vary from state to state, it is usually uncommon for a prescription to be written for oral anovulants covering more than a one-year period. In some places, three or six months is the norm.)

4.   Is a woman's decision to use an oral anovulant an artifact of the knowledge and advice she obtains from the media and her friends, or more a function of her doctor's encouragement (who also obtains his information from trade journals and drug detailmen)?

5.   How do women weight 1) safety; 2) risk (short- and long-term); 3) effectiveness; 4) cost; 5) convenience; and 6) availability?

6. Is the main question one of giving the woman control over her reproductive destiny, her health, her life? Or is the real question how far society is willing to go to reduce its fertility, at whatever the individual and social costs?

When pregnancy is defined as a disease, the above questions take on special significance, for there is an urgent and disjointed societal response which tends to disregard the broader socio-cultural context within which therapeutic decisions might otherwise be couched.

Diethylstilbestrol as a Special Case

Why ought we direct our attention to one specific drug, diethylstilbestrol (DES), when the drugs themselves are really not in question here? I think the answer has to do with when the bill (alluded to earlier in the quotation from Lasagna) comes due — who shall pay it, *what will the bill demand of us* (as individuals or as a society), and what services have in fact been rendered?

DES is of special interest here because it has been shown to submit its bill within a fairly well-defined time span, because its claims are unreasonable in exchange for what has been proferred, and because it focuses our attention on a fundamental question which, until now, we have avoided asking: If unanticipated effects are what we fear or seek to avoid, or known effects what we seek to minimize, does not the whole issue become a question of the sensitivity of our receptors for recognizing that harm has been done or is likely to ensue? The mere fact that evidence of little or no harm is variously apparent or obscure seems frivolous in light of our knowledge about how harm can be redefined or manifest in ways at present unknown. We are at the crossing point of becoming alarmists, on the one hand, and progressive (i.e., willing to take calculated risks) on the other. Is it *really* important to study *how much* radiation is needed to harm the human system, or *how much* malnutrition interferes with the mental and behavioral development of a child? We already know the answer without calculating the "effects" to the nth degree! But such calculations have often served to obfuscate the valid issues, and to create a facade that *something* is being done to redress a social, medical or political evil. I contend that those "somethings" are not what is needed. We are our own worst enemy, and we need proof; but where do we look for that proof, and is it possible to obtain it?

A look at DES enables us to clarify some of the questions raised above, none of which are rhetorical, and few of which have been considered by those in power or those astute enough to make us uneasy and inquisitive.

Peter Greenwald, writing in the *New York Times* (February 23, 1973), contends that DES should not be expanded to contraceptive use until more comprehensive work has been done. As the director of New York State's Health Department Cancer Control Bureau, Greenwald stated that the FDA's approval of DES for "emergency" use as a "morning after pill" was "unfortunate" and would encourage wider use despite the risks involved with the controversial drug. His comments were made during testimony before the Senate Labor and Public Welfare subcommittee on health, *"which is investigating practices of medical research using humans."* [Emphasis added.] Others seem to be equally concerned with questions of social toxicity, although they may not be aware that their psychological discomfort is a consequence of these nagging issues, which transcend simple cause-effect relationships in clinical applications of pharmaceutical techniques.

Although these issues will be detailed later, it is significant that Greenwald argued:

Because of a 'definite cancer risk to daughters born of pregnancies where DES was taken, it seems likely that widespread use of DES as a morning-after pill will result in some daughters born with this vaginal cancer risk, either because of an excessive time lapse between conception and DES prophylaxis, or because other forms of treatment fail.'

⚹ [While DES is useful in the treatment of some disorders such as breast and prostate cancer, Greenwald believes its uses should not be expanded until more comprehensive research has been done.]

Jane E. Brody, writing the same day in the *New York Times* (February 23, 1973), explains that the controversy over DES extends to use and testing of any drug in the United States. She breaks down the issues into the following components:

1. [The]... difficulty of weighing benefits versus risks when the benefits are immediate and the risks may be decades off, and when the *"patients" are essentially healthy.* [Emphasis added, based on our original premise that pregnancy has been defined as a disease, and what that

implies for therapy.]

2. [The]. . . inability of the FDA to prevent the use of a marketed drug for an unapproved purpose or to enforce restrictions on approved use, and the financial, organizational and legal obstacles to adequate testing of drugs under a proprietary system.

Brody observes that an FDA official stated in the fall of 1972 that the FDA had been unable to interest any drug company in conducting controlled studies of DES as a contraceptive.

By last year [1972], tens of thousands of women — mostly college coeds — had been given DES as a morning-after pill, even though it had not been approved for this use, and most of the women were not participating in an FDA-approved research study.

Why is this unusually problematic? Without going into too much detail, let us examine the setting. DES is a manmade chemical possessing many properties of the natural female sex hormone, estrogen. It has been approved by the FDA for many years for the treatment of menopausal symptoms, swelling of the breasts following childbirth, cancer of the prostate, and certain uterine disorders, and can also be used to speed the fattening of chickens and beef cattle. From all outward appearances, we seem to have happened upon a true panacea! But there are a few more questions.

In the fall of 1972, the FDA banned the use of DES in animal feeds, as a result of a Boston report demonstrating that vaginal cancer had been found in eight girls whose mothers had taken DES during pregnancy to prevent possible miscarriage ("a use of DES which had never been proved to be effective"). Since the initial report, over 100 cases of vaginal and cervical cancer in daughters of such women have been officially reported. How many more have gone unreported? Is the safety of a drug to be determined so definitively simply as an artifact of our cancer registries? But there is more to come.

FDA's approved labeling for DES states that it may be used for contraception "provided the patient is offered the option" of an abortion should pregnancy occur. The label further specifies that a pregnancy test should be done first, and if positive, DES is contraindicated. The label goes on to read that DES is "to be considered as an emergency treatment only and not as a method for birth control with continuous or frequently repeated therapy." It is up to the prescribing physician to define "emergency," for as a spokesman for the FDA observed, "For us to [define emergency] would be to interfere with the practice of medicine." Thus, by default, the physician's judgment determines the medical and social outcomes of each DES prescription written. That is the law.

A major problem facing the FDA and the public is that the FDA is presently unable to enforce its caution against "frequent" use of DES; any licensed physician can prescribe any amount as often as he sees fit. Given the nature of the evidence to be discussed in chapter 4, this becomes an awesome responsibility.

Similar caution regarding time span during which standard oral contraceptives may be used safely "was widely ignored by physicians."

Anita Johnson of Ralph Nader's Health Research Group claims that the term "emergency" has no meaning. She argues, Brody notes, that more women will now take DES with fewer safeguards, "citing a study that indicated that many women given DES were not told of its potential hazards, were not adequately followed-up and were not screened for factors that might make them peculiarly susceptible to adverse side effects."

This literature, though limited, will be reviewed with special attention to the anticipation of untoward side reactions that may lie decades in the future and which, given the interrelationships between the individual and society, may threaten the viability of society's adaptive mechanisms.

The Law as a System of Control

Jaffe (1969: 406) believes that "medical men want to experiment, and the public approves of experimentation. An occasional catastrophe will touch off a public outcry [e.g., thalidomide] with consequent over-reaction, but on the whole the public continues to finance and to applaud medical experimentation and discovery." Jaffe continues:

The objective of our quest is a system of concepts, standards, and rules governing human experimentation that gives due recognition to the various interests entitled to protection.

I would suggest that "the various interests entitled to protection" includes us all.

Acknowledging the work of Calabresi, Jaffe observes (p. 407):

> The law often approves of institutional and personal conduct that, statistically considered, creates threats to life or limb. [In general], the threat is to persons unidentified at the time the risk is created.

It is curious that some question exists about the role of our legal institutions in furthering and safeguarding the interests of those involved in human experimentation. If not the law, what other institution is capable of this? The irony is that no separate body of law exists for the adjudication of these very important issues involving human rights and the protection of what society holds dear. Jaffe (p. 407) informs us:

> There is not as yet much law explicitly dealing with human experimentation, but the common law [by which we mean the law devised and administered by the courts] has developed and continues to develop doctrines that are applicable.
> . . . These doctrines can be devised and applied by the judges with considerable flexibility so as to accommodate the interests of subject, experimenter, and collectivity.

On page 408, Jaffe continues:

> The advantage of the common law judicial control is its flexibility — a characteristic consonant with the presently fluid condition of ethical attitudes toward experimentation. *Ad hoc* judicial decisions, it is true, may mean a stiff judgement for damages against an individual who learns only after the event the precise application of the rules governing his conduct. . . . There have been, as a matter of fact, few lawsuits concerning the legality of experimentation.

Chapter 8 will consider most of the litigation that has been adjudicated involving oral anovulants, together with the rationales that have been employed, given the "fluidity" of the attitudes alluded to above; bear in mind that the law also reflects the social currents of the times, and as such, is dynamic while often appearing to be inert.

PREGNANCY AS A DISEASE

The Role of Regulation

It should be apparent that the role of law, the role of regulation, and ethical standards interact to provide the infrastructure within which human experimentation is conducted, new pieces of technology are developed, old pieces of technology are perpetuated, or abandoned, and *people* are allowed to live out their lives in relative security, health, independence, and spontaneity. Regulation is juxtaposed with the role of law for conceptual purposes, but also to clarify areas in which the two fail to touch or overlap, and at times appear to be at odds with one another. The FDA does not view human experimentation as does the common law, nor do physicians view experimentation in the same way as their patients. How these different perspectives and doctrines complement and contrast is vital to our understanding of what is happening to us and around us. Regulation, by definition, implies standards, recipes, control, deference, expertise, and stratification. It is not to be ignored, and we can depict the institutional frameworks through which regulatory processes are manifest. In this manner, can we criticize its shortcomings, and opt for greater propriety and sensitivity in those arms of society entrusted with regulating what happens to us, our children, and generations yet unborn? We turn to bodies of ethical standards, regulatory statutes, and institutions lying outside the immediate realm of the individual, who, acting alone, cannot protect or advance himself as well as when he acts in concert with others sharing common beliefs, values, aspirations, and experiences.

Regulation and law are thus checks and balances on society's propensity toward entropy, or disorganization over time and space, and are essential in the management of information necessary to assure survival of culture under varying demands.

Regulation in the drug industry involves not only the production of pharmaceuticals (e.g., quality control, what is produced, their distribution), but also the drug industry's tendency to evolve goals frequently at odds with those of society at large. Not surprisingly, then, the drug industry seeks to alleviate pain, to prolong life, to ease the burdens of the aged; but a fundamental question remains to be asked — are these noble goals amenable only to pharmacologic solutions, or are other approaches effective, safe, more germane, and apt to result in fewer societal repercussions?

Contraceptive Practice

Certainly it is useful to know the parameters of the problems being addressed, and the informed citizen will know what oral anovulants are, what they do, how they act, who takes them, and the likely consequences of their use. We shall consider the development, testing, distribution, evaluation, and use of oral anovulants in the United States and abroad.

Contraceptive Side Effects and Contraindications

These will be distinguished from the foregoing discussion in light of the pharmacological knowledge and tradition of American medicine; recall that these drugs were developed and administered through the medical institutions, and their effects have in most cases been examined from the clinical perspective, and that alone. This is not intended to be a sourcebook on clinical aspects of oral anovulants, but I believe it is important that we examine the clinical and nutritional effects of these powerful synthetic drugs in order to get a better handle on their likely societal impact. The question might be, why do they exist at all?

Contraceptive Labeling and Advertising

The uniqueness of oral anovulants from the standpoint of how demand for them has been created was mentioned earlier, and it is important that we consider the evolution of labeling and advertising pertaining to their sale and distribution. Regulations exist in this realm, as well, since the FDA has seen fit to specify caution and particular formats for educating the physician and the consumer. Truth in advertising and thorough and prompt reporting of new adverse effects and contraindications are imperative.

Questions remain about the rapidity with which this information can be communicated; about the rationality of depending upon the pharmaceutical manufacturers for unbiased reporting; about alternative sources of information for physician and patient. Finally, there is the question of what to do with this information, and who is to decide. Are the advertisements read, are labels sufficient to provide the physician and the patient with requisite warnings and instruction on the proper use of these drugs? Do they make any difference in the long run, since it is the existence of the drugs and our propensity to use them that is being questioned here? Would revisions in advertising and labeling help, or would they serve only to "oil the machine," which should not exist as such in the first place? These would lead to outward changes in the setting of drug use, without concomitant changes in the reality or the rules of the system.

Ethics of Experimentation with Human Subjects

We are fortunate in having a number of ethical codes to refer to for guidance in this area, for if we accept the argument that all therapeutics is experimentation, ethical factors cannot be overlooked. A number of the major ethical codes will be surveyed, to provide insight into whether oral anovulants represent a tolerable intrusion on the lives of many millions of women, according to established principles of research and practice. Graubard writes in the Preface (1969: v):

While it would be impossible to set a date when systematic study of the matters discussed in this issue first received wide attention, some would say that substantial inquiry began to be made soon after World War II.
Out of a concern with the violence done to human beings came an interest in defining precisely the conditions under which human experimentation might take place.

He continues on page *vi:*

There is reason to believe that ethical issues will increasingly preoccupy social scientists, and not only because of a growing resistance to their research proposals.

5

SOCIAL DEMOGRAPHY AND
TECHNOLOGICAL INNOVATION

Although the issues touched upon briefly in the preceding pages are real and worthy of our attention, it cannot be stressed strongly enough that there is another side of the coin. World-wide emphasis on population numbers and growth rates tends to divert attention from the rampant political, social, and economic disparities that contribute to population pressure being considered a social problem of great magnitude. Simply lowering the fertility rate does not result in more goods and services for more people. Reduction of socio-economic inequities might better precede mass campaigns to reduce growth rates, so that sufficient attention is directed toward the societal context within which decisions about family size are made; otherwise, family planning can provide only the ad hoc measures to ameliorate what poverty and failure to progress in fact mean to a society. Premature concentration on contraceptive programs may reduce the impact of population pressure, which could be instrumental in encouraging governments to address needed social and economic reform.

Noting that family planning can be used as a substitute for structural change in society, Mamdani (1972: 17) quotes Dudley Kirk, a neo-Malthusian:

Given the favorable attitudes found in surveys, family planning may be easier to implement than major advances in education, or the economy, which require large structural and institutional change in the society as a whole.

This utilitarian, reductionistic response typifies the stance taken by many population "experts" in the voluminous literature on family planning.

The more immediate questions, I believe, revolve about, not methods of overcoming seeming resistance to family planning programs, but the too ready proclivity to seek easy solutions to complex problems which, by their very nature, are social and thus not amenable to ad hoc "stabs in the dark" that fail to address the true issues at fault in society's organization and institutions. Only after this has been done ought we turn to biological or "natural" phenomena in the hope of affecting the residual problems that go beyond our ability to prevent or correct via socio-cultural mechanisms.

This argument can best be illustrated by analogy to the control of a disease such as tuberculosis — and again, I contend that pregnancy is defined as a disease. We need only look at the success of TB programs in controlling the disease to see that one does not initiate such programs by examining the attitudes of individuals exposed to the risk of contracting TB. Such an approach would do little to correct the environmental and organizational deficiencies (e.g., housing, chronic infection, malnutrition) that predispose individuals to TB. We ought to begin by studying the *organization* of health and medical care services; only afterwards should we move to reduce pockets of resistance to social measures by focusing on characteristics of individuals (literacy, age, sex, marital status, occupation) to explain the balance of the population that continues to show a disproportionate share of TB.

The same argument can be applied to family planning where the alleged goal is to reduce population growth rates. Demographic characteristics are simply not sufficient to explain why some women successfully adopt and use contraception while others either fail to show interest, discontinue use, or employ a contraceptive method improperly. In this sense, oral anovulants are no different from barrier methods of contraception. However, at this point the various methods diverge, and oral anovulants take on greater complexity and societal impact, for the risks and implications arising from their use are correspondingly more substantial.

Mamdani (1972: 19-20) offers the following insights, which reinforce the above argument:

If population control is to be a substitute for fundamental social change, then the theorist must look at the population "problem" *independently* of other aspects of social relations. It also follows that he must look at motivation as individual motivation, independent of the individual's social existence. If one understands it as an *attitude,* then the emphasis will be on the social reality in which this attitude originates. But if this finding is understood as a fact, stripped of its relation to other social phenomena, then the origin of this "fact" in social existence will be totally obscured, and it will be seen only in the thinking of isolated individuals. The result will be an emphasis on surveying the opinions of these individuals, as in the KAP surveys, rather than on understanding the basis of the opinions themselves in their social context. The solution will be to disseminate contraceptive devices and to "educate" individuals about the importance of using them, rather than to seek to alter the social circumstances and thus to change the social basis of the individual act.

Mamdani (p. 51) states that "a people will be receptive to a form of technology [any technology] only if they stand to benefit from its introduction." He emphasizes that "those who pay the cost of change do not necessarily reap its benefits. . . . [T]he major assumption of the 'overpopulation' theorists that people should associate their poverty with their large numbers and thus seek to limit their numbers in the face of adversity [is not valid]. The crucial question is, would such a response be rational?" (pp. 105-106).

Dorothy Nelkin (1973), in her excellent volume entitled, *Methadone Maintenance: A Technological Fix,* provides the background for the discussion to follow. While her book is about methadone, I argue that we can substitute almost any other drug or piece of technology and change barely a phrase; like the present effort, it is a case study — the faces change, but the show is the same every night.

Nelkin (pp. 4-6) describes technological innovation in this manner:

The controversial development of methadone maintenance and the problems of individual programs suggest the complex issues involved in the use of technology as a quick solution to profound social problems.

A technological approach requires that a task be precisely defined and the objective clarified. Once objectives are determined, the relative advantages of alternative solutions can be weighed, and the most appropriate selected.

"Right straight through our history we have adopted a policy that invention, technology, ingenuity, resources, ought to be available to deal with anything we want to have dealt with." [quoting Margaret Mead]

She continues on page 61 to reinforce what I have been contending from the very beginning:

a technological solution does not confront the real social and/or psychological problems that lead people to addiction in the first place. These critics view it as no more than a simple medical approach to a complex social, political, and psychological problem. It is criticized as a short-sighted patch-work treatment based on the principle of least effort, and one which "deepens prevailing mystifications by perpetuating the drug means for the solution of human problems."

The question then becomes (Nelkin, 1973: 3):

To what extent can social problems be circumvented by reducing them to technological problems? Can we identify quick technological fixes for profound and almost infinitely complicated social problems, fixes that are within the grasp of modern technology and which would either eliminate the original social problem without requiring a change in the individual's social attitudes, or would alter the problem as to make its resolution more feasible?

Is this not what we are attempting to do in the realm of family planning technology and application? Of course, the distinctions are blurred and categories of thought are not mutually exclusive, but, Nelkin continues (pp. 140-143):

Societal and individual values are increasingly counterposed in almost every medical act. Some rational and just order must be established between these values to ensure the good of society while safeguarding the traditional rights of the person. This is the central ethical issue before contemporary medicine. . . . Can we make optimal use of medicine as an instrument of social good without illicit intrusion on individual human rights?
. . . the limitations of the procedure and the dangers in relying on a narrow technological approach . . . [occur within the] context of "crisis" [and] a primary objective becomes rapid and visible evidence of "success."
Success becomes defined in the instrumental language of statistics. . . .
[Methadone maintenance is] less expensive than other therapeutic approaches. . . . In addition it draws appeal from the compelling authority of research and the dramatic success of medical science in managing disease.
The possible long-term physiological or psychological effects, about

which knowledge remains fragmentary and controversial, and the implications of social control tend to be overshadowed by the short-term social benefits and the efficiency of a technological solution. *Regulatory agencies must trade off the values of careful scientific evaluation of the effects of a new agent against public demands for immediate use of a promising if incompletely understood drug.* [Emphasis added.]

Nelkin believes that physicians tend to resent the power exercised by the FDA as a threat to their professional prerogatives. She notes (p. 145):

Concern with control perpetuates an incongruous legal status. . . . This vague differentiation between therapy and research has raised ethical problems which are not . . . unique to methadone maintenance. Earlier experiments resulting in therapeutic innovations – from the discovery of vaccination in 1798 to experimental heart transplant surgery – have raised similar problems. For clinical research in therapeutic innovations usually draws upon a population of patients who are often desperate to try a new "cure." In this context, where those volunteering to be subjects stand to benefit from the experiment, the principle of voluntary and informed consent that was established to protect the subject of experimentation has a restricted meaning.

As Jaffe pointed out earlier (1969), there has been surprisingly little legal precedent specifying the degree to which the civil rights of a patient may be violated by a given clinical procedure. Social policy and law are inextricably related and recognized as such by the legal system.

I suggest once again that when pregnancy is defined as a disease, certain formalized routines are set in motion; techniques otherwise reserved for traditionally defined disease are employed; attitudes toward risk/benefit ratios are conditioned along the lines of standard therapy, and, as Nelkin (pp. 147-148) observes:

The peculiar problems of long-term medical relationships are of growing importance, as illnesses such as arthritis, hypertension, and overweight increasingly become subjects of medical consideration. Doctor-patient relationships are generally based upon the expectation of short-term illness; the patient is expected to cooperate with the doctor and staff, relying on their expertise and observing the rules they set regarding his particular definable disease.
While the pharmacological aspects of the process may achieve certain ends, the more costly but crucial aspects of social rehabilitation are rejected.

PREGNANCY AS A DISEASE

Technological management of social problems is itself a problem involving the disaggregation of the difficulty into components of manageable size; this presupposes a well-defined disease or technological problem, without giving adequate attention to the long-term impact of the solution in other spheres of existence, perhaps even unknown at the time of the intervention.

Pregnancy as a disease. The concept admittedly is unusual — perhaps even repugnant to some — but I believe we ought to give it some thought. What does such a definition mean for an individual, a family, a child — a society? Does it imply that a fetus is not unlike a headache, a tumor, or an infection? Can you love or learn to love such a product of conception — or the pregnancy itself, as long as the condition is likened to a pathology? There is already some precedent — hopefully now on the wane — whereby menstruation is considered a sickness, disgusting, something to be endured but not talked about; simply recall euphemisms young girls, women, and their mothers used for the "period." Why not apply the same emotions and revulsion for something closely related — pregnancy and childbirth? Instead of taking blackberry brandy or Midol, take an oral anovulant. It is simply a matter of substitution, or is it? All that is different, really, is that the female must now obtain a prescription from a physician. A pill is a pill. Cheap. Quick. Easy. Clean. We take them all the time, for upset stomachs and pneumonia and influenza. The importance of the label is not to be underestimated, but the societal ramifications are no doubt difficult to document. Once you have mixed an omelet, you can never again retrieve the individual eggs. The synergism has produced something greater than the sum of its parts. Whether pregnancy is in fact *defined* as a disease, or simply *treated* as one, probably makes very little difference. The interface of medicine, technology, ethics, and law is currently a philosophical "No Man's Land" because we have lacked the methods and concepts necessary to comprehend it — we have simply let it unfold.

6

THE ORAL ANOVULANTS

History

No history of oral anovulants would be complete without an understanding of the social context within which they were developed. While this is discussed in numerous texts on reproductive physiology, contraception, and biochemistry, the single most comprehensive source is found in the Final Report prepared for the National Science Foundation (March 19, 1973), entitled *Interactions of Science and Technology in the Innovative Process: Some Case Studies.* In the Introduction (p. 1-1) the authors write:

Technological innovation is the nexus that joins science, technology, commerce, and industry. *Innovation is both the sum and the result of the complex operations through which the inventive, scientific, and entrepreneurial genius of modern society produces social and economic impact on that society.* [Emphasis added.]

This chapter will detail the development of this form of therapeutic innovation, and consider if the availability of oral contraceptives is "potentially epochal." To oral anovulants are attributed the following effects:

The oral contraceptive has played a significant role in liberating women from involuntary childbearing. The use of oral contraceptives also affects the number of women participating in the labor force and is gradually altering the attitude of employers concerning the promotion of women into positions of greater responsibility.

No mention is made of the social reform necessary to bring about the changes in opportunity structures that underly social development.

Etzioni and Remp (1972) are also curious about this issue. They ask, "Can new technologies be used to reduce significantly the costs and pains of needed social change and to accelerate its pace?" They note that "shortcuts deal only with the symptoms of the problem and not with its fundamental causes." Contending that "our effectiveness in handling social problems is most likely to be increased in the near future through the utilization of technological means," Etzioni and Remp believe that "all shortcuts which 'work' are much more effective for some subpopulations than for others," and they quote Alvin M. Weinberg, then director of the Oak Ridge National Laboratory, who wrote in 1966 (pp. 2-3):

In view of the simplicity of technological engineering, and the complexity of social engineering, to what extent can social problems be circumvented by reducing them to technological problems? Can we identify Quick Technological Fixes for profound and almost infinitely complicated social problems, "fixes" that are within the grasp of modern technology, and which would either eliminate the original social problem without requiring a change in the individual's social attitudes, or would so alter the problem as to make its resolution more feasible?

This question of feasibility and effectiveness fails to address the real problem — "fixes" connote stopgap, ad hoc measures taken to reduce the immediacy of a particular threat or problem, leaving their ultimate resolution to future thinkers who may be more capable of dealing directly with them; i.e., persons who will not "circumvent" the causes and implications.

It becomes important how "information about the value of technology is generated, assessed, and used. This question can hardly be separated from ones . . . [of effectiveness since there almost never is] a clear answer if a technology 'works' or not, and the decision if it 'works' is much affected by the *societal context in which knowledge is produced, communicated and used.*" [Emphasis added.]

Etzioni and Remp (p. 153) further concede:

[T]he proposed shortcuts deal only with the symptoms of the problems and do not get at its fundamental causes that they are only illusory solutions and cannot really handle the problems.
The word "shortcut" evokes an image of superficiality, or non-
structural, illusory solutions.
A shortcut simply means a shorter way of getting to the same place.
Or, viewed more abstractly in terms of costs, the use of fewer resources,
less psychological strain, and less effort to achieve a stated goal. . . . it
might be useful to compare technological shortcuts *not to ideal and
unattainable alternatives, but to available strategies.* [Emphasis added.]

Four alternative approaches are presented to the solution of
social problems (Etzioni and Remp, 1972: 154-168). They consist of:
1) the Liberal Reformist Approach; 2) the Psychotherapeutic Approach;
3) the Rationalistic Approach; and 4) the Revolutionary Approach. The
fourth alternative is the one that best fits the case of the oral anovulants, and is described as follows:

Conceiving of social problems as an illness, and of shortcut remedies
as the treatment of symptoms of this illness, provides a way of intro-
ducing some distinctions which may help considerably in reaching a
more subtle definition of the issue at hand.
The dangers of treating the symptoms without attempting to eliminate the underlying processes of the disease itself have been discussed
by Dr. Howard Rusk. As he notes, an aspirin may relieve the symptoms
of a fever, but also may allow an associated disease to destroy vital
organs.

The same logic can be applied to the treatment of social disease, as well:

Too often the focus is on the disturbing symptoms of social unrest,
unhappiness and conflict. Today the symptoms are the use and abuse
of drugs.
By this view the fundamental questions to be clarified with regard
to the reduction of drug addiction are not those concerned, for example, with the addictive or non-addictive properties of drugs; rather,
the fundamental problem is the recognition and removal of the conditions which prompt individuals to use drugs. Accordingly, the main
purpose of any investigation of domestic problems shoud be the discovery of the social conditions that give rise to these symptoms of
disturbance.

. . . if we refer to the relative effectiveness of the social system in the handling of its problems, and to the society's realization of its values, then we can identify the same difference between societal aspirins, which have an immediately alleviating effect, and remedial actions of more basic significance. [Emphasis added.]

Etzioni and Remp (p. 169) continue:

"[S]ocial palliatives" or "social aspirins" suggested initally that as a consequence of relieving distress of the overt symptoms of the disorder it will become possible to ignore the underlying problems and accordingly they will receive less treatment than they would otherwise. [On the other hand,] . . . it is not evident that the use of social palliatives or social aspirins necessarily inhibits more basic remedial actions. . . . it is possible in many instances that "symptomatic treatment" may be a *necessary pre-requisite* to a more basic attack on the problem.

There are, of course, difficulties in making accurate social diagnoses, and the successful treatment of one symptom is no assurance that another will not appear at some other point in time and space:

Science is always an unfinished enterprise . . . *For instance, the birth control pill, up to a certain point in 1970, was very widely considered safe by the public as well as by doctors and most medical researchers. However, suddenly, a flurry of reports appeared indicating that, even though the pill had been used by millions of people, there was no conclusive evidence available as to its effects, and a whole new set of questions about the safety of the pill arose.*
It follows that the scientific input into the policy-making processes on these questions is inevitably tentative and always given to revision from internal scientific sources.
. . . The evaluation of birth control methods is a case in point. . . . If a birth control method is judged effective only if all chance of conception is eliminated, then the research design can be very simple. All that needs to be done is administer the technique and then check for any births [or conceptions] thereafter. [Emphasis added.]

But certainly, the effectiveness of oral anovulants is but one consideration, and that is why I devote so much space to this analysis.

THE ORAL ANOVULANTS

The Social Significance of Oral Anovulants

While research and development leading to the availability of oral anovulants began in 1951, other forms of contraception have been available for thousands of years. Presently, conception can be controlled through a number of techniques of varying safety, effectiveness, cost and ease. These methods include sexual abstinence, prevention of the sperm from reaching the ovum, incapacitation of the sperm, and control of ovulation (NSF Final Report, 1973: 10-1). The mode of operation of oral anovulants is suggested by their placing the female in a state of castration, thereby inhibiting the possibility of fertilization of the egg. Oral anovulants do in fact place a woman in a state of what has been termed "pseudo-pregnancy."

The NSF case study notes that more than 20 million women currently ingest oral anovulants. "The dollar value of the market for oral contraceptives is nearly $200 million and is growing rapidly, especially in developing countries. The two major innovators – Searle and Syntex – have reaped rich rewards for their creativity and willingness to take risks. Each has developed into a multihundred-million dollar company, from a relatively small base, since it introduced oral contraceptives" (p. 10-1).

Social and historical development of oral anovulants can be approached from a variety of perspectives, although I believe that for present purposes, tracing the evolution of the biochemical and physiological underpinnings would be superfluous. For the reader seriously interested in the step-by-step emergence of the chemical components of oral anovulants, there is no shortage of textbooks and journal articles detailing their discovery, investigation, refinement, and classification. This aspect is most closely associated with the field of biochemistry and the development of the pharmaceutical industry from its infancy in the nineteenth century.

In very brief commentary, let me simply list the sequence of events that have led to the currently marketed products, bearing in mind that these drugs are in a state of continuous development and change, both with respect to dosage and chemistry.

Development has taken place over the past 30 years, and the NSF Final Report (1973: 10-12–10-13) summarizes the "Decisive Events" as follows:

1. A. Butenandt, et al., Europe and U.S. (1934), described the structure of progesterone.

2. A.W. Makepeace, et al., University of Pennsylvania (1937), discovered hormonal inhibition of ovulation.

3. H.H. Inhoffen, et al., (Germany, 1938), synthesized ethisterone, the first orally active progestin.

4. R.E. Marker, et al., (Pennsylvania State University, 1941), converted diosgenin to progesterone. Production of progesterone from diosgenin made steroids inexpensive and stimulated considerable research on chemical derivatives that would have been virtually inaccessible otherwise.

5. R.E. Marker, Mexico (1944), founded Syntex to produce hormones.

6. M. Ehrenstein and W.M. Allen, University of Pennsylvania (1944), demonstrated progestin activity of 19-norprogesterone. This discovery provided the first structural modification of progesterone that retained its activity.

7. A.J. Birch, et al., Europe (1949), developed a simplified synthesis of 19-norsteroids.

8. C. Djerassi, Syntex (1951), synthesized norethisterone.

9. F.B. Colton, Searle (1951), synthesized norethynodrel. Djerassi and Colton, share the honors for synthesizing the compounds actually used in most oral contraceptive products. Each put together the observations of Ehrenstein, Inhoffen, and Birch, and became a major inventor of the oral contraceptive by that combination.

10. Mrs. S. McCormick and Margaret Sanger, Planned Parenthood Federation (1951), requested from G. Pincus and the Worcester Foundation for Experimental Biology a proposal on contraceptive methods. By providing the incentive at the right time to the right people, they contributed greatly to the rapid success of the development of the oral contraceptive.

11. G. Pincus, Worcester Foundation (1951), proposed the development of an oral contraceptive.

12. M.C. Chang, Worcester Foundation (1953), evaluated the inhibition of ovulation by 19-norsteroids and various means of administration. Although both Syntex and Searle knew that they had compounds with excellent endocrine profiles, it was Chang who evaluated the products in the major application, proved their efficacy on animals, and paved the way for clinical tests.

13. G. Pincus, Worcester Foundation (1954), proposed the concept of

cyclic control, a concept that enabled the product to be a psychological success by providing assurance that the user of the oral contraceptive is not pregnant. Without cyclic control, the product would have had a much more difficult time passing Food and Drug Administration regulations and being accepted by a mass market.

14. G. Pincus and G.D. Searle & Company (1954), undertook commercialization of the oral contraceptive. . . . Syntex was not yet powerful enough to undertake such a major commercialization by itself. Therefore, without Searle's decision, this major development might have languished for years.

15. Searle (1960), introduced Enovid as an oral contraceptive. With approval by FDA, the marketing of this product marked the culmination of the innovative process.

The NSF Final Report acknowledges that this innovation was "need oriented," a direct response to the initiative of the project sponsor, G. Pincus.

A few points worthy of our focused attention do not appear from the summary above.

Rock's Evaluation

Both Searle and the Worcester Foundation approached Rock in 1954, contending that they had a clinically effective product. A population of women was needed who were infertile but who ovulated regularly. A large-scale enterprise was needed to demonstrate the safety and effectiveness of the oral contraceptive. *"Due to the anticontraception climate in Massachusetts, it was decided to employ Puerto Rico as a providing ground"* [Emphasis added.] (NSF Final Report, 1973: 10 – 10).

When Rock's evaluation on human volunteers found the product safe and effective, it was natural for Searle to cosponsor the Puerto Rican trials. The company had to overcome *the traditional ethical pharmaceutical company doctrine that drugs are given to cure disease.* The notions that contraceptives are somewhat disreputable or that there would be protests and boycotts against oral contraceptives also had to be overcome. Attitudinal surveys were not conducted; rather, the oral-contraceptive development had a *momentum that overcame such objections.* [Emphasis added.]

The Puerto Rican research was aided by Dr. Celso-Ramon Garcia, who left the University of Puerto Rico to join John Rock in Boston. After some small-scale trials in Boston, Garcia assumed major responsibilities for the Puerto Rican phase initiated in 1956 with Enovid. "At first there was concern over the relatively large number of side effects that were attributed to use of the drug. Later studies showed that the power of suggestion was producing a large percentage of the reported side effects." These were, of course, only those side effects that were at the time measurable, and immediate, and apparently no attention was given to whatever other effects the use of this drug would have on participating populations.

Food and Drug Administration Approval

The FDA approved oral anovulants on two separate occasions; the first, in 1957, was for treatment of menstrual disorders, on behalf of both Searle and Syntex. The second approval came in June, 1960, for use as contraceptives. Searle received this in 1959. Syntex received delayed approval for its analogous drug in 1962, primarily because Parke, Davis and Company's refusal to enter the oral contraceptive business forced Syntex to find another licensee. The Ortho division of Johnson and Johnson agreed to provide this function, and Ortho-Novum was marketed in 1962. Later, Parke, Davis and Company entered the market with Norlutin.

Use of Oral Anovulants

While the extent of adoption of contraception, and the oral mode in particular, is variable across the world's populations, and the reliability of statistics characterizing the propriety of usage is equally problematic, some information is available. As one might expect, considerably better data exist for the developed nations and their populations than for the less developed countries of Latin America, Africa and Asia. Jones and Mauldin (Population Council, 1967) have made an admirable effort to synthesize information on the developing world.

Aside from the personal inclinations of target populations, considerable differences occur with respect to national policies governing

THE ORAL ANOVULANTS

the manufacture, import, distribution, advertising, and practice of oral (and other forms of) contraception (IPPF Europe, 1973).

An illustration of the expanding popularity of oral anovulants is provided by Van Keep (1967: 1):

TABLE 1

**Estimated Number of Cycle-Packs Sold
Yearly per 1000 Fertile Women**

Country	1959	1960	1961	1962	1963	1964	1965	(est.) 1966
USA	16	22	79	251	409	812	1178	1524
Australia			122	349	937	1707	2346	2796
U. Kingdom			4	25	72	251	426	500
Belgium				31	140	230	485	781
Brazil				7	24	109	228	383
Colombia				11	78	224	375	682
France				20	25	34	79	134
W. Germany				24	31	201	279	378
Italy						1	20	59
Spain						6	42	72

Van Keep calculated the values of Table 1 according to the following argument:

The figures for the total number of women in each country were obtained from the demographic yearbook of 1964 of the United Nations. The number of fertile women, both married and unmarried, was calculated arbitrarily taking 38 percent — the world average — of the total number of women.

From these figures an impression of the number of Pill-users per 1000 women can be obtained by dividing the number of packs sold per year by 13 since, in general, 13 packs are required for one year of oral contraception.

Van Keep's figures represent a very crude approximation, since there is currently no way to establish: 1) the number of pill-packs actually used by the purchaser; 2) the true number of fertile women in a given society; 3) how the packs were used or broken up and possibly lost, or stolen, or shared by others; 4) the figures from the *Demo-*

graphic Yearbook are not always reliable; 5) a woman may not take pills over an entire year, or she may do so sporadically; 6) pills are acknowledged to be widely available in Latin America without prescription,* and there is likely to be a black market or other uncontrollable distribution of these drugs; 7) we cannot gauge how many of the purchasers were planning to use these drugs for themselves, for contraception, and with proper therapeutic intent.

Allingham (1970: 31–41) has attempted to improve on the accuracy of earlier studies investigating the adoption of oral anovulants among American women (e.g., Ryder and Westoff, 1967; Allingham, Balakrishnan and Kantner, 1969), focusing on married women in order to give greater precision to the population exposed to the risk of adopting oral contraception. He concluded that: 1) the rate of increase in the proportion of women using oral anovulants has declined since January, 1966; 2) the two major factors responsible for the initial burgeoning use of oral anovulants — the new marriage cohorts and "the rapid adoption of orals among earlier cohorts at later durations" — have diminished impact; 3) concern over possible health hazards of oral anovulants is a real deterrent to substantial new oral anovulant adoption; and 4) under current conditions, the maximum oral use rate will be much less than one.

Allingham's findings are interesting, when examined in the light of Gerrard's (1964: 208-209) Presidential Address to the British Medical Association, in which he commented on the proclivity of patients to take matters into their own hands with respect to requesting and using certain medication that is potentially detrimental to their well-being:

Is it any wonder, therefore, that knowing all this, many doctors are extremely unhappy nowadays about the growing tendency among patients to want to prescribe for themselves, and, moreover, to ask for drugs to fulfill their social as well as their medical needs.

The reason is perhaps that over the years, thanks to the Press, the

*Dr. Charles C. Edwards, Commissioner of the Food and Drug Administration, stated in 1970 while appearing before a subcommittee of the Committee on Government Operations that, in response to a question about sales of pills without prescriptions: "We have no direct evidence of this, although we have been informed by a number of sources that it is occurring at a far greater degree of frequency than we would like. We have not been able to get hard facts on it."

radio, and television, people have become so much better informed, and in many ways this is a very good thing.

. . . There is also the question of the oral contraceptives which are becoming so popular nowadays. One realizes, of course, that from the patient's point of view this method of contraception has certain attractions. The trouble, however, is that many people, including myself, are doubtful whether, over long periods, the use of this type of contraception is wise.

. . . These pills, which contain two types of hormones, are used to suppress ovulation, and the bulk of evidence so far available goes to show that they do this by depressing a secretion of the pituitary, which may be described as a master gland, situated at the base of the brain and linked up through the blood stream with a group of ductless glands to which the gonads belong. This, in turn, has an effect on the ovary, and the result is that ovulation does not take place. *The snag is what was previously a balanced mechanism has now been disturbed.* Does it matter? In the short term there has not as yet been much evidence that it does, and many doctors, including myself, use preparations of this kind quite often in the treatment of gynaecological disorders, such as dysfunctional uterine bleeding and endometriosis.

Recently, however, there has been evidence to suggest that these tablets should not be taken by diabetics, and as there is a similar link between the pituitary and the pancreas, which is another member of this group of glands, this naturally makes one wonder if they will prove to be safe in the long term. Indeed, it may be many years before we shall really know, perhaps not until large numbers of women who have taken them for this purpose over long periods of time have passed through the menopause. *Meanwhile, it should be understood quite clearly by everyone, and I include husbands here, that if women take drugs of this kind for social rather than for therapeutic reasons they are taking part in a mass experiment – call them guinea pigs if you like.* . . . It is this particular method which I have my anxieties about. My worries are, of course, shared by a large number of doctors, and many warnings of this kind have been given before. Unfortunately, however, people tend to believe what they want to believe, and therein lies the rub. [Emphasis added.]

In an editorial appearing in the *Southern Medical Journal* (May, 1970), the pill controversy was discussed from the standpoint of the impact Senator Gaylord Nelson's Hearings on the safety of oral anovulants (1970) have had on use of these drugs. The Hearings apparently brought growing public concern to the point where physicians were being increasingly questioned about the safety of this mode of contraception. "According to a Gallup Poll reported in *Newsweek* February 9,

1970, 18 percent of the women using the pill had abruptly stopped using it and an additional 23 percent were 'giving serious consideration to quitting.'"

We do know that millions of Americans are interested in practicing contraception, and that the mass media and increasing sophistication and education of the general public have made these men and women more aware of the risks and benefits to be derived from the use of these drugs. Naturally, many are concerned over the adverse publicity attending the Hearings mentioned above – but the concern appears to lie mainly in the domain of clinical changes and imbalances, and not so much in the realm of social and cultural ramifications. This is to be expected, for their bodies are more immediate, their lives are here and now, and perhaps only a sociologist would consider the social linkages that *may* occur in unanticipated ways some years hence. Besides, the readily quantifiable changes of clinical medicine are easier to deal with than the conceptual disaggregations and social "waves" found when applying one's sociological eyes to foreign subject matter. The questions are important, not only because of their heuristic value, but because of the immensity of the public involvement: "It is estimated that 8 or 9 million women in the United States are using the pill. This is roughly 18 percent of all the women between the ages of 15 and 45" (p. 608).

One of the most interesting pieces of research is a study conducted by R. Levin, A.I. Jowett, and A.G. Raffan, which looked at "Conception Control in Doctors' Families"; with the controversy raging in the courts, among the legal, medical, and regulatory institutions, in the press, over backyard fences – what do *doctors* do? Do they have the courage of their medical convictions? In a study conducted in November, 1969, *before* the British Committee on the Safety of Drugs made their well-known findings public, 2,490 letters and questionnaires were sent to a random sample of general practitioners aged 50 or less, together with all consultant obstetricians/gynecologists, drawn from four regions of Britain. Of the original sample, 743 replies were received, or 30 percent on the average. Of the 743 who returned their questionnaires, 641 (86 percent) were married and 102 (14 percent) were single. Only the answers of the married respondents are recorded in Table 2. Focusing on the methods of contraception used by the physicians and their families, Table 3 is very informative.

THE ORAL ANOVULANTS

What can we conclude from Table 3 with respect to the contraceptive practices of the sample?

1. The percentage of physicians' families using oral anovulants is significantly higher than in the general British population (approximately 16 percent of British women "at risk" use oral anovulants); there are significant differences in the use of the oral mode by region.

2. The percentage using no method of contraception compares with the general population, although coitus interruptus (about 4 percent) is much less than the general population.

TABLE 2

Age Distribution of Those Who Replied

Age	Number	%	Spouse's Age	Number	%
Under 30	60	9	Under 30	119	19
31–35	117	18	31–35	149	23
36–40	132	21	36–40	143	22
40+	332	52	40+	230	36
Total	641	100		641	100

TABLE 3

Analysis of Contraceptive Practices

Method	All married respondents N=641	Region			
		South	Midlands	North	Scotland
	%	%	%	%	%
Oral C.	27	26	31	23	25
Condom	27	26	26	27	30
None	16	14	19	19	16
Diaph.	16	22	13	13	10
Steril.	8	7	7	7	10
Rhythm	6	7	4	6	9
IUD	6	6	5	4	7
Coitus Int.	4	2	1	7	4
Other*	4	2	6	5	5

*Not specified: also note that percentages total to more than 100 because some households use more than one method.

3. The investigators concluded that the percentage employing sterilization is higher than they expected (8 percent), and while a comparable figure is unavailable, only about 0.2 percent of British males aged 16 to 50 are estimated to have resorted to vasectomy.

4. It is believed that the condom is less frequently used (27 percent) than in the general population, while the intrauterine device (IUD) is probably used more often than in the general population (6 percent).

5. The use of the diaphragm and the rhythm method is probably very similar to that found in the general population.

Table 4 disaggregates the use of contraceptive method by "importance of preventing pregnancy."

TABLE 4

**Analysis of Methods of Contraception Used in
Relation to Importance of Avoiding Pregnancy**

	All married respondents N=641	Importance of Preventing Pregnancy			
		Imperative	Important	Does not matter	Already Pregnant or trying
	%	%	%	%	%
Oral C.	27	8	13	3	3
Condom	27	7	15	3	2
None	16	1	1	9	5
Diaph.	16	5	7	2	2
Steril.	8	4	2	2	–
Rhythm	6	2	3	1	–
IUD	6	2	4	–	–
Coitus Int.	4	2	2	–	–
Other	4	2	1	1	–
All married respondents	–	29	44	18	9

The investigators concluded that those answering "imperative" or "important," but using no contraception, were all in the upper age bracket and their wives most likely post-menopausal. A couple of additional points of interest are the following: 1. Some 73 percent of all married respondents reported they regard pregnancy avoidance as "imperative" or "important."

THE ORAL ANOVULANTS

2. The oral anovulants and the condom are the methods most heavily depended upon by those desiring a high degree of reliability; the diaphragm was also reported frequently. There were even a few instances where *both* the oral anovulant and the condom were used.

Table 5 presents answers to the question of whether oral anovulants had ever been used in the past, or were currently being employed. We observe that more than half of the respondents had used oral anovulants in the past, or were presently doing so; we also notice significant variation among the different regions, ranging up to 64 percent in the North.

Those in Table 5 who reported never using oral anovulants – 48 percent – were then asked why. Significantly, physical harm (e.g., thromboembolic disease) was the major single reason; Table 6 provides a breakdown of the responses:

TABLE 5
Use of Oral Contraceptives

	All married respondents N=641	Region			
		South	North	Midlands	Scotland
	%	%	%	%	%
Used	52	50	64	44	48
Not used	48	50	36	56	52

TABLE 6
Reasons for Not Using Oral Anovulants

Reason	Respondents Never using N=309	Region			
		South	Midlands	North	Scotland
	%	%	%	%	%
Contra. husband's resp.	7	6	3	8	11
Worried about physical harm	45	50	35	44	34
Religious pref.	6	6	6	10	3
Medically cont.	14	14	16	14	11
Other	34	27	40	24	41

Table 6 suggests that "other" reasons were important and the investigators report that these reasons consisted of a distaste for routine medication, and that sterilization had been performed prior to consideration of oral anovulants.

Those persons who had at one time used oral anovulants but had discontinued their use are described in Table 7. Without doubt, "minor side effects" was the most common reason given for discontinuing the use of oral anovulants, although "fear of physical harm" was especially important in the southern region. An earlier survey conducted in 1968 cited fears about long-term safety (58 percent), compared with 30 percent reported in the table. Within the "other" category, the present report noted that a large percentage (45 percent) discontinued oral anovulants because of conditions not considered to be minor, e.g., depression and thrombotic disease.

TABLE 7

Reasons for Discontinuing Oral Anovulants

Reason	Married Respondents Discontinuing N=160	Region			
		South	Midlands	North	Scotland
	%	%	%	%	%
To become pregnant	24	29	16	20	33
Preferred IUD	8	12	4	8	7
Fear of physical harm	30	43	20	24	27
Minor side effects	46	46	48	48	40
Other	45	41	34	48	67

Among the 160 who responded to the question in Table 7, the condom, sterilization and the IUD were more frequently used among those who abandoned the oral mode than among respondents as a whole.

THE ORAL ANOVULANTS

Finally, respondents were asked, if the wife had used more than one brand of oral anovulant, why had she switched? Table 8 gives us the answers. "Minor side effects" was the largest reason given, with a desire to obtain a lower dosage/potency ranking next.

TABLE 8

Reasons for Changing Brand

Reasons	All answering N-188	Region			
		South	Midlands	North	Scotland
	%	%	%	%	%
To obtain lower dosage/potency	32	37	31	25	33
To obtain different hormonal balance	16	11	18	19	22
Greater reliability	2	2	–	–	3
Minor side effects	59	52	61	69	58
Other	30	16	18	12	92

The most significant findings concern the observation that at the time of the study, in November, 1969, the use of oral anovulants was greater among physicians' wives than in the general population. The reasons why must be left to speculation. One plausible explanation is derived from the high value placed by the respondents (73 percent) who desired to avoid pregnancy. Levin, Jowett, and Raffan conclude (p. 699) that:

The over-all impression gained from the survey is that doctors and their wives — whilst scientifically more knowledgeable than their patients — are every bit as human in the ways they face the problems and opportunities of family life.

Weil (1972) appears to corroborate the above statement by acknowledging (p. 52):

In writing and lecturing I have learned that people hear what they want to hear and tune out what they do not want to hear. The practice is most damaging [probably because of the example they set and because of what such poor logic implies for their perceptions of reality] in groups that regard themselves as free of preconceived notions, such as physicians and pharmacologists.

It is probably reasonable to assume that what doctors do in their own extra-professional lives has a bearing on their approach to patients; and of course the possibility remains that what doctors do with respect to their patients overlaps into their social lives, as well.

It is unfortunate that so much of what has passed for social science fits Weil's interpretation of irrelevance. He notes on page 53:

When you ask a question in research and the data come back in this unhelpful way — that is; sometimes yes, sometimes no, most of the time it makes no difference — *you have asked the wrong question.* [Emphasis added.]

Excerpting from an earlier comment by Weil on page 53, the issues are not of drugs, but that,

there are no facts. Or, more precisely, there are no facts free of value judgement. Everything we hear and read about drugs is affected in this way, all facts about drugs are merely masquerading as such. And the problem is likely to be most serious in just those cases in which it appears to be absent. The pharmacologist who "just gives the facts" is often distorting data through biases so sweeping and so internally consistent that they remain invisible and unconscious.

We must constantly search for new and alternative ways to address reality — the *reality* of drugs, their use and *presence* — concentrating on the *settings* in which their impact is *manifest* and *interpreted.* And yet this very thing, a new way of thinking, leads us to distrust or fear levels of consciousness that have perhaps remained untapped. As Weil (p. 53) stresses:

[In evaluating the "usefulness" of a concept] The aim of scientific inquiry is not to reveal absolute truth but to discover more useful ways of thinking about phenomena. Our ways of thinking about drugs leave us unable to describe, predict, or control the phenomena associated with drugs except in the crudest ways, as the insoluble drug problem demonstrates. Insoluble drug problems of this sort always indicate erroneous, useless concepts. I believe we can literally think our way out of the drug problem by changing the concepts from which it arises — the outmoded ways of thinking about consciousness.

The outward forms of reality, the exoskeletons of the drug phenomena, have tended to preoccupy our attention to the disregard of the infrastructure and infraprocesses that are, in fact, at the root of our social and scientific dilemmas.

However, if we liken the human frailties of our trusted scientific professionals to those of the earlier practitioners and pharmacologists briefly discussed in the section on the pharmacologic mode of therapeutics, we see through Weil's eyes (p. 58) how allopathic medicine has contributed to our biosocial "blindness." Allopathy is the western model of medicine, defined in *The Random House Dictionary* as "the method of treating disease by the use of agents, producing effects different from those of the disease treated. . . ." The basic rationale derives from *the treatment of disease through counteracting its symptoms.* Again — have a headache? Do not reduce the stress causing it or engage in more restful behavior — take an aspirin. Do you suffer from heroin addiction? Substitute methadone. Are you an alcoholic? Antabuse is better than Canadian Club. Is your per capita real income uncomfortably low? Counteract with a birth control pill; this saves wear and tear on the polity and economy that would be the consequence of social change and reorganization. And so the story goes, with the endless search for a new and improved social aspirin. Weil observes (p. 58):

Modern allopathic medicine is essentially materialistic. [Even if one subscribes to the germ theory of disease.] We live in a world full of germs, some of which are correlated with physical symptoms of infectious disease. But only some of us get infectious diseases, and we get them only some of the time. Why? Because there are factors *in us* that determine what kind of relationship we will have with those germs that are always out there — a relationship of balanced coexistence or one of unbalanced antagonism.

What Weil is saying — or perhaps implying — is that even clinical disease in the technical sense of the term (disease) has both psychic and physical components (e.g., is psychogenic), and social problems (e.g., population and ecology), *defined* as "disease," must be addressed recognizing that *the pathology so defined cannot be "treated" as though it were unidimensional.* The "population problem," or the "ecological crisis," or the avoidance of conception are not amenable to solutions administered in pill form, or through a hypodermic needle, or in a paper cup. To continue to attempt such reductionistic, ad hoc approaches can logically lead us only to delay and frustration.

And because allopaths have no grip on the true causes of disease, they cannot prevent us from getting sick; they can only treat our acute problems. (Weil, 1972: 60)

He continues (p. 62):

The problem is not that things have this ambivalent nature, but that our ordinary consciousness, however, is perfectly capable of substituting a *both/and* formation for the *either/or* of the ego.

If we are willing to follow the reasoning that brought us to this point, questioning the merits of allopathic models of medicine and humanity, then what is *non-allopathic* medicine or setting? One problem is that the success of non-allopathic medicine is not always readily apparent. So we cannot as easily employ immediate indicators of response to this mode of thinking and therapeutics. "[M]any non-allopathic healers ignore symptoms totally. Treatment of symptoms, however sophisticated, focuses the patient's attention on symptoms. This reinforces the anxiety and other negative feelings that helped produce the symptoms in the first place. An important first step [in non-allopathy] is to distract the patient from his condition" (Weil, 1972: 64). The second step is to motivate the patients (be they individuals or a society — remember the setting) to heal themselves. This entire rethinking requires that we *use our minds* to extricate our bodies and our social selves from those situations which we define as pathological. A chemical is no substitute for reason; it never has been, and is unlikely ever to be — nor is the surgeon's knife, or the engineer's machine.

Are we to conclude that it is irrelevant to consider the use of oral anovulants from the standpoint of traditional toxicity and pharmacological and clinical dilemmas? That is a pretty strong statement, given that oral anovulants "work," are used by millions of women who *appear* to live their lives with no *outward* signs of incapacity, and questions of "social toxicity" are theoretical issues that do little more, at present, than make us hesitate along the course we are following. Is the real controversy becoming clear? It is *not* simply that some women die or are permanently disabled through use of oral anovulants – or *any* drugs, for that matter. It is *not* that more thorough research into the side effects and contraindications is not in the offing. It is *not* that some religious sects object to the practice of contraception. It is *not* that the FDA, the courts, and the medical profession are indecisive, profit-hungry, power-seeking, malevolent institutions bent on self-aggrandizement at the public expense. It is *not* that prescribing these drugs for sexually immature females may lead to premature closure of the epiphyses. In fact, the real controversy is all of these things, and perhaps none of them, in that drugs and every form of technological innovation have tended to make us concentrate on the symptoms of our social problems to the neglect of underlying organizational deficiencies that are products of perspectives or views of reality that go deeper than present methodologies research. I contend that the controversy derives from a basic misunderstanding of the contents, of the *rules,* that direct our behavior and philosophies, that result in outcomes unanticipated at the time we attempt to enter our model of reality and change it. An analogous situation would be if, given a lump of protoplasm, we could not possibly foresee its ultimate realization in a human being, if we could not understand the role of the genetic *code* instrumental in bringing about the transition from lump to person. At the societal level, we have even less knowledge about the analogous code – the setting's rules – which transforms social action into something greater than the sum of its parts. What socio-cultural indicators, in criticizing current methodological approaches, are more likely to provide the data needed to better direct our destinies through a more realistic understanding of what we are as humans? The fact that we *do* this, or *do* that, as individuals or as aggregations, should tell us something about the way natural forces impinge on our deliberate behavior, but I contend that knowing this is not sufficient.

Taylor (1970: 23) asks, "What are the alternatives?" He continues:

Greater risk of pregnancy due to use of less effective contraceptive methods is certainly no alternative. *However, an alternative method of pharmacological contraception is available.* [Emphasis added.]

Can we be doomed to live again the mistakes of our long, pharmaceutical past? Instead of going *beyond* the constraints of our thinking that lead us to a conception of reality based on *attributes* of the setting, we immediately seek new solutions that are in fact the same as those that failed in the past: the substitution of one drug for another! Instead of asking what social organizational innovations can be implemented to ameliorate or prevent an evil, we search in desperation for a "more effective" social aspirin. In the foregoing example, Taylor refers to the substitution for estrogen-progestin compounds of prostaglandins, "Upjohn's 90-day injectable medroxy-progesterone acetate." Clearly, this is another example of an ad hoc measure, and implies, if this drug does not work (or is unacceptable for a variety of reasons), *let's try another one!* In the reductionist philosophy of the allopath, we are thus temporarily placated by the knowledge that "the most prominent undesirable feature will undoubtedly be that most women will prefer to take their medicine by mouth rather than by injection." Why question the original oral anovulants? Because, in Taylor's words:

Results of a retrospective study [never the best kind] conducted in 48 hospitals in five major cities of the United States suggest that users of oral contraceptives have a 4.4 times greater risk of suffering a thromboembolic episode than do non-users, and the risk is the greatest for those taking sequential pills. These findings are similar to those reported in Britain. A British study found the hospitalization rate from cerebral thrombosis and embolism for women age 20 to 44 to be 47 per 100,000 among oral contraceptive users compared with five per 100,000 among non-users. An etiological relationship between thromboembolic disorders and the use of oral contraceptives seems to be established, but *the incidence is still exceedingly low and certainly is not of sufficient magnitude to begin to overbalance prophylactic or therapeutic benefit being employed by oral contraceptive users in general.* [Emphasis added.]

An editorial appearing in the *Southern Medical Journal* (1970: 608) shows a glimpse of recognition of the problem's true nature:

For the doctor who is asked about the safety of the pill it is well to keep in mind that there are other satisfactory methods [of contraception]. Even though other methods are not 100 percent effective [as the pill is for all practical purposes], their effectiveness varies with the diligence of the user, and before the introduction of the pill many couples carried out satisfactory family planning. It should always be emphasized that the pill should be used only under medical supervision since it is potent medication having side effects which can be serious for a small percentage of patients. Indiscriminate prescribing by physicians and indiscriminate dispensing of pills by pharmacists is a problem which should be dealt with by the appropriate medical and pharmaceutical organizations and the Food and Drug Administration.

The major clinical side effects of oral anovulants have been described above. Additional effects include serious nutritional and behavioral disorders; the other "potentially" harmful consequences of this mode of therapeutic intervention are those that threaten the resiliency of society by reinforcing short-cut, technological solutions that are inappropriate for the complexities and qualities of social behavior. The question becomes, can a society endure if its control over its environment is so dependent upon what comes out of a bottle? Problems of mal-distribution of resources, conflict, differential access and reward, negative externalities, and illiteracy cannot be corrected or prevented if our first response is the medicine chest. Oral anovulants tend to reinforce our affinity for simplistic models of human beings.

Kistner (1971), a strong proponent of oral anovulants, caustically remarks:

Only one birth control measure is safer than the Pill — total sexual abstinence. And that has never been a popular choice. . . . But, over the past decade, many anti-Pill factions have developed, some medical, some theological, some political. . . . The "Pill impasse" presents the nation's policymakers with a dilemma of social policy. If they take the Pill off the market, it means a possible setback for the whole movement of population control, at least until women learn to transfer to other contraceptive measures. But what method will provide equal efficacy? Unfortunately, it is not a simple task to devise a substitute for the Pill — that is, a substitute of equal effectiveness, without side effects, lacking metabolic derangements and with a built-in crystal ball to tell us what the effects will be 20 years hence.

The clinical side effects occurring and perceived by the world's women who have taken the oral anovulants or are at risk of doing so may be a mixed blessing. They have been instrumental in focusing on the logic and desirability of this pharmaceutical product, and they have placed the use of these drugs on the public agendas of most nations.

PREGNANCY AS A DISEASE

Everywhere, people have some opinion, informed or otherwise.

Use of Oral Anovulants in Developing Countries

Jones and Mauldin (1967) have done a superb job of analyzing the role of oral anovulants in the developing nations, noting (p. 1):

[O]ver the last two and one-half years, the consumption of oral contraceptives has grown much more rapidly in the developing countries [by 2 and ½ times] than in the developed countries [by about 90 percent]. This trend is likely to continue. . . . There has been a burgeoning interest in the pill in lower-income countries as the price has progressively declined.

It is undoubtedly difficult to measure acceptance rates because of lack of data; while pills have been available in some developing countries for many years, in other nations there are people who have never heard of them. "At the present time, there are very few studies in which the acceptance of oral contraception can be gauged in relation to a clearly specified segment of the female population" (Jones and Mauldin, 1967: 3). We do know, however, that oral anovulants tend to be used with greater frequency among IUD dropouts than among the general population. "With only a few exceptions, the studies from the developing countries show that 20-30 percent of those accepting pills drop out during the first cycle, i.e., do not return a second time." (It is interesting to note the finding of Frank and Tietze that 1.4 percent of women who accepted supplies of pills never took one of them; in a Taiwan study, the corresponding figure was 7.4 percent.) Clearly, most terminations are due to adverse side effects; but we might have expected this, and it is not at issue here. The fact that a substantial number of users of oral anovulants drop out, especially within the first three cycles of use (Jones and Mauldin, 1967: 11) suggests that they have made a choice to accept the risk of pregnancy or some other "less effective" mode of contraception in exchange for the oral mode. It is questionable whether they all have made this choice on the basis of informed consent. The side effects may have been sufficient to cause this abrupt change of behavior; on the other hand, a study reported in *Family Planning Digest* (March, 1972: 13-14) contended that family planning clinics in New York City teach their patients much less than they need to know, and it is unlikely that the situation is any better in the developing countries alluded to above. "Furthermore, the knowledge patients have is 'not directly related to the instruction given in the respective clinics'." There is considerable variability among patients, and it is difficult to pinpoint the reasons why patients continue or drop out. Family planning clinics are notorious for not informing their clients of contraindications associated with oral anovulants, and:

Living as we do in an age of instant communication, the Columbia investigators . . . [believed] that a patient's ability to cope with "frightening and incorrect stories concerning fertility control techniques such as the pill" depends in great measure on the degree of rapport and trust already established with her physician or clinic personnel.

Kutner (1972) investigated the relationship between fear of pregnancy and use of oral anovulants. The Fear of Pregnancy Test (FOPT) was administered to 1,325 female patients using various contraceptive methods, who claimed they were currently exposed to sexual intercourse, and not pregnant. The women using birth control pills, when contrasted with 24 pre-contraceptive pill patients, as well as with the rest of their group, were not found to be significantly less afraid of pregnancy than any of the other contraceptive users (e.g., IUD users, rhythm method users, surgical users); however, four groups — rhythm method users, IUD users, surgical users, and non-contraceptors — were less fearful of pregnancy than were pill users.

These issues deserve our attention. Lasagna (1968: 139), commenting on the national publicity being generated over clinical side effects of oral anovulants, puts the matter this way:

All the complications described are known to occur in people who do not use oral contraceptives. No new diseases have been seen. Why, then, the concern over the possibility of a cause-and-effect relationship? It must be remembered that the suspicion of alert physicians is almost always the first indicator of pharmacotherapeutic mischief. Rarely can the doctor do more than suspect a cause-and-effect relation between drug and toxic effect, since hardly any drug's side effects are unique to that drug. Further, massive pulmonary embolism, strokes, and heart attacks are relatively rare in young women.

Whether these women are aware of the similarities and differences in the risks they are assuming, either by risking pregnancy or by taking an oral anovulant, is another question. The same changes brought about by oral anovulants with respect to blood clotting also occur during pregnancy. But they do not occur when a woman is not pregnant, nor do they occur when some other means of contraception is employed. The role of oral contraception and lactation, especially in the developing countries, has prompted considerable discussion in the nutrition literature. Not only is the compound passed through the placental barrier to the fetus, but there are recorded instances of infants being born with gynecomastia (enlarged breasts); in each case, however, the condition has disappeared, leaving no adverse effects, in about three days. Oral anovulants are transferred to the breast-fed infant, although there are apparently no overt, long-term effects. I include these points only to suggest other areas where the pharmaceutical mode of therapeutics can overlap into areas where the effects or consequences may appear only indirectly, in another place and another time.

The Focus on the Female

Even an astute observer such as Barbara Seamon (*Free and Female,* 1972: 218-219) seems to miss the point:

If you doubt that there has been sex discrimination in the development of the pill, try to answer this question: Why *isn't* there a pill for men? . . . [It is because] women have always had to bear most of the risks associated with sex and reproduction. Therefore, governments and scientists reasoned, it would be all right to substitute one risk for another. One still hears this argument from certain doctors . . . who like to point out that the risks connected with the pill are less than the risks of pregnancy.

The question is not whether a male or a female "pill" should be encouraged; we are all human beings. The focus on the female has been unfortunate, I concur, but whether a pill should be the one best solution for either sex is the real question. Nobody should have to submit to this type of manipulation, however effective it is in preventing a pregnancy, when there are other ways of doing things. Developing a pill for men would do nothing to address the basic problem; it would merely shift the focus to a different person, while the underlying social insult would remain fundamentally the same.

Further Comments

There are many ways of approaching the subject of contraceptive use, and oral anovulants, in particular. I have elected to disregard intensive discussion of the details of contraceptive usage, since adequate literature exists for the reader who has special interest in family planning and related components of contraceptive side effects and contraindications. Entire volumes are devoted, for example, to the effects of oral anovulants on protein metabolism, carbohydrate metabolism, folate metabolism, vitamin, mineral, and electrolyte balance, liver function, and diabetes. But the present inquiry attempts to synthesize the major threads of these disciplines that have one thing in common — the use of irreversible technology in pursuit of the redress of social evils. We are, in the process, harming people and cultures in ways which we lack the ability to appreciate fully at the present time. The following chapter will discuss DES as a special case, and is included only to illustrate the tragedy of our tactics.

7

DES
AS A SPECIAL CASE STUDY

Why the Concern?

Adenocarcinoma of the vagina is rare in young girls, usually occurring in women age 50 and older (Herbst, Ulfelder, and Poskanzer, 1971: 878-881). However, between 1966 and 1969 at the Vincent Memorial Hospital in Massachusetts, eight girls between the ages of 15 and 22, who had been born in New England hospitals between 1946 and 1951, entered the annals of medical history when they were diagnosed as suffering from this unusual tumor. Seven of the eight mothers involved had taken diethylstilbestrol (DES) during their first trimester of pregnancy years earlier; a retrospective study indicated that DES appeared to have increased the risk of adenocarcinoma in the offspring of these women, with symptoms not appearing until 14-22 years later. Since this time, over 200 cases have been documented and 20 deaths recorded, largely through the efforts of Nader's Health Research Group.

Herbst, Ulfelder, and Poskanzer's (1971) findings were corroborated by Greenwald, and by George Linden and Brian E. Henderson (1972) who reviewed the California Tumor Registry data for the period from 1950-1969 to see if there had been a comparable increase in the incidence of adenocarcinoma in young adults and adolescents during the same period. Table 9 presents the results of their inquiry. The data reflect relative increases in the age group from 10 to 19 years for cancer of the vagina, corpus uteri, prostate, testis, and bladder. Since Linden and Henderson also examined the data for cancers of the breast, bladder, stomach, colon, and rectum, they concluded that similar increases were not registered for these sites.

TABLE 9

Cases of Cancer According to Site, 1950-1969

Site	Period	All Ages	Age 10-19
Vagina	1950-1962	224	0
	1963-1969	260	4
Corpus uteri	1950-1962	4,075	1
	1963-1969	4,337	4
Prostate	1950-1962	8,207	0
	1963-1969	6,785	3
Testis	1950-1962	570	22*
	1963-1969	751	53**
Bladder	1950-1962	3,942	0
	1963-1969	3,712	7

*(Age 10-14=0)
**(Age 10-14=5)

In the age group 20-24 years, relative increases were demonstrated for cancer of the vulva and testis. Linden and Henderson were unable to conclude whether their findings were due to chance fluctuations in the incidence of the disease, although they acknowledge that their findings were compatible with those of Herbst, Ulfelder, and Poskanzer, and those of Greenwald, regarding the possible linkage between cancer and DES.

The First Recorded Case of Transplacental Chemical Carcinogenesis

Stilbestrol is a synthetic nonsteroid estrogen known to be carcinogenic. It must be emphasized here that none of the oral anovulants contain stilbestrol and that the synthetic estrogens present in them are steroidal.

Knowing the suspected links between stilbestrol and cancer developing in the offspring of mothers who took DES during the 1940s to prevent miscarriage, can we shrug and say, "More research is needed?" I am afraid that such a response is to be expected in the medical profession, where the first response to such suspicions tends to be framed in such questions as, "Cannot we find a 'no effect' level of this carcinogen which would permit us to continue to use the drug?" In other words, do not remove the drug from the social system; simply attempt to *reduce the dosage* so that fewer cases of cancer are likely to occur.

In an article entitled "DES: A Case Study of Regulatory Abdication" (*Science*, 177), Nicholas Wade informs us:

DES is a chemical of bizarre and far-reaching properties, chief of which is that it is a spectacularly dangerous carcinogen. Some 22 countries have taken steps to ensure they do without DES in their food supply. The hormone is a regular ingredient in the American diet because the federal government permits its use as an additive in cattle feed.

Hearings before Senator Kennedy's health subcommittee brought to public attention deficiencies in the FDA and Department of Agriculture (USDA) systems of protecting the American consumer from harm from DES. The hearings pointed out some shortcomings in using scientific information for regulatory decision making, and demonstrated that the law and the regulatory doctrines are inadequate to the task.

The FDA first approved DES for use in fattening cattle in 1954, specifying that it be withdrawn from the cattle feed 48 hours prior to slaughter so that none would be present in the meat. The FDA was responsible for developing techniques to detect the presence of DES in meat, and it fell on the shoulders of the USDA to inspect the meat. Eleven years passed with neither agency checking meat for DES on a regular basis; this was not simply an oversight:

[For] . . . in 1959 the National Cancer Institute recommended that "it would seem the better part of reason to exclude this known potent carcinogen from our diet and *to eliminate such food additive practices as have been shown to lead to any detectable residues . . . in our food.*" [Emphasis added.]

Thus, the sensitivity of our measuring instruments became crit-

DES AS A SPECIAL CASE STUDY

ical, since in 1959 it was possible to detect DES residues in poultry but not in sheep or cattle. Significantly, the Delaney Anticancer Law of 1958 is unequivocal in requiring that no known carcinogen be used in food; the FDA had to ban the use of DES in poultry feed. Shortly thereafter, methods were developed to detect DES in beef and mutton, but not until 1962 did the FDA *do* something; Congress moved to neutralize the Delaney law with regard to DES, and wrote a new clause known as Section 512 (d) (1) (11) of the Food, Drug, and Cosmetic Act, allowing DES to be used as cattle and sheep feed as long as no residue is left in the meat when the carcinogen is used in accordance with label directions that are "reasonably certain to be followed in practice" (Wade, 1972: 335).

In other words, if you find DES in meat, that's the fault of the farmer for disobeying the "reasonable" regulations. *So don't ban DES, jail the farmer.* [Emphasis added.]

N.S. White, a USDA meat inspector in Los Angeles at the time, wrote a scientific paper critical of the lack of strictness in controlling the use of DES. He was censored by a USDA personnel officer and subsequently quit the USDA. White's article was published following his departure from the agency.

The USDA's initial detection method was capable of picking up DES in meat down to levels of 10 parts per billion (ppb). In 1964, the year before, DES had been shown to cause tumors in mice when fed at a level of 6.5 ppb, and the "no effect" level has not been determined to date. Nevertheless, DES continued to be used without regular testing and control *for another seven years!* As a matter of fact, the FDA's testing became progressively less stringent: the USDA tested 495 samples in 1967, 2.6 percent containing DES. In 1968, the USDA sampled 545. In 1970, the sample had diminished to only 192 cattle.

It appeared that 1971 was a turning point, since the USDA tested 6,000 that year, but strangely, no DES was found.

That, at least, is what USDA Assistant Secretary Richard Lyng told Senator William Proxmire (D-Wis.) on 31 August. The truth was that DES had been detected in ten animals, in quantities up to 37 parts per billion, but a lower official had ordered these results to be suppressed. The explanation proferred when this became known was that the residues were not to be reported until confirmed by a second method of analysis. No second method was available, so the result had not been reported. In his letter of apology to Senator Proxmire, Lyng called the episode an "inexcusable error" and a "gross malpractice."

It became apparent that there was a determined effort on the part of our regulatory agencies, such as the FDA and the USDA, to evade the consumer protection mandates of Congress, and this was brought home in April 1971 when the first cases of transplacental chemical carcinogenesis were reported. But even this recognition was not sufficient to change the system's trajectory:

The FDA's response to the crisis . . . was not to ban DES, but to lengthen from 2 to 7 days the mandatory period between the withdrawal of DES from a cow's feed and the time of the animal's slaughter.

DES continued to be discovered in cattle following the "new" directive, for two possible reasons: 1) it took longer than seven days to clear the animal's system; or 2) some cattlemen continued to break the law by failing to withdraw DES from feed prior to slaughter. Apparently, "a cattleman had just about the same chance of being caught — about 1 in 5000 — whether the withdrawal period was 2 days or 7." The evidence of the safety margin of seven days was flimsy, at best, and many cancer experts believed that much more deliberate action was needed to prevent the ingestion of DES. In spite of this, FDA Commissioner Edwards claimed:

We are absolutely convinced that, if we do have and enforce sound controls, DES can be used safely and effectively.

Roy Hertz of the Rockefeller University has suggested that the only justification for using DES in cattle would be the threat of famine; but given that "the present wheat surpluses are the highest in a decade [except for the now infamous wheat deal with the Soviet Union], even though farmers were paid $1 billion this year [1971] not to grow wheat."

There is some agreement that anything that "adds to man's carcinogenic burden should be eliminated if possible." Political speculation on the FDA's recalcitrance to ban includes the Administration's concern with rising meat prices — "the banning of DES would cause a small but perceptible rise — 3.85 cents per pound — in the price of beef," the FDA's fear that strong action taken against DES would lead to questioning of many other chemicals currently not being debated in the public press, and that the FDA simply cannot admit that it has been wrong.

Miller (1971) has written an informative editorial detailing the etiological and epidemiological determinants of cancer in prenatal humans, citing the following evidential sources that may be instrumental in preventive oncology. He includes: 1) the occurrence of congenital cancers *in utero;* 2) high incidences of perinatal mortality due to cancers of the same cell type as occur prenatally (e.g., teratoma, neuroblastoma, primary liver cancer, Wilms' tumor, and leukemia); 3) the concomitance of certain cancers and congenital deformities, the latter developing from early embryo-genesis; and 4) an increase in childhood leukemia related to high maternal age or low birth order. In brief, cancer may be inborn in a variety of ways. However, three questions are brought to our attention: 1) What other cancers can be induced by stilbestrol? 2) What other clinically used chemicals cross the placental barrier and may cause cancer? 3) How can we recognize these tumors?

Miller's main point is that we can reduce the risk of cancer through improvements in our cancer registries, and more intensive interaction between prospective epidemiological studies covering suspected carcinogens and the work of the laboratory experimentalists. He, too, fails to recognize the role of drugs, *per se,* and our approach to pharmacotherapeutics, which is the real issue here. Must we await the appearance of cancer, and develop sensitive diagnostic procedures in the interim, or would it not be better to minimize the associated risks inherent in drug therapy and intervention by looking at the reality of the therapeutic setting (and not simply the setting's outward manifestations and effects) in pursuit of alternatives *not requiring drugs in the first place?*

The Use of Women as Guinea Pigs

Women have become increasingly vulnerable to exploitation and possible physical harm in their rush to obtain greater control over their bodies and prevent unwanted pregnancy. Onieal (1973) notes that in the search for improved means of mechanical and chemical contraception, "the effectiveness of the contraceptive method over its safety and side effects" has been emphasized to the neglect of untoward individual and societal consequences.

Pregnancy as a disease. Bearing in mind our earlier discussion of allopathic medicine, it is not surprising that the FDA approved DES as an "emergency" contraceptive on February 22, 1973; the drug meets all of the qualifications of standard therapeutic intervention, and is prescribed, taken, and accepted as though conception were pathological in the same sense as a urinary tract infection.

DES contains a massive dose (25 mg.) of synthetic estrogen, and is administered twice a day for five days; it is believed to show anti-fertility properties by preventing implantation of the fertilized egg in the uterine wall. The daily dose is some 500 times the amount of estrogen a woman normally has circulating in her body, and the fact that the drug is synthetic implies that the compound is not identical to the natural estrogen her body produces. Consequently, its presence cannot be considered *natural*, either in quantity or quality. What are the probable consequences of this therapeutic measure? Probably something quite unlike maintenance of the body's normal homeostasis and function. Its carcinogenic properties, after 19 years of circumvention, denial, distortion, and regulatory neglect, have finally been accepted by the FDA and the USDA, and as of January 1, 1973, DES can no longer be used as an additive in cattle feed. In the period preceding this landmark and long overdue decision, much has happened, the most significant events — presently known — being the induction of vaginal and cervical cancer in adolescents and young women. If the cancer has not progressed too far, *other* medical technology such as surgery and radiation therapy will probably permit these unfortunate women to live. Of young women who have *not* been included in the current list of 100 plus, tragically, many will die, because their cancer will go unrecognized due to ignorance or the neglect, for whatever reasons, of pelvic examinations and Pap tests necessary to detect cancer at a sufficiently early stage of its development. Who shall pay this bill? First, the young women who had no control over their destinies. They will pay the highest price, whether or not they survive. Second, their mothers will suffer, perhaps not direct physical consequences, but certainly anguish and guilt over their role — albeit that of agent — which resulted in the horrendous outcomes only now coming to our attention, the death or perhaps permanent incapacity of their offspring. Third, we all share in the expense, in that our society has facilitated and perpetuated similar untoward outcomes for our people because we have not been willing to concede our ignorance of the consequences of our interventions. We *do* know that most forms of human cancer take between 10 and 30 years to develop; we *do* know that the "nuisance" side effects of drugs – especially DES – such as nausea, dizziness, headaches, and vaginal bleeding, are more than temporary discomforts tolerated in exchange for protection from miscarriage, pregnancy or some other undesirable experience. They are symptoms telling us that we are doing much more than we think, as the body rebels at this intrusion on its natural sanctity. On the one hand, we elect to ignore these outward signs that the body is being violated, *in the hope* that they will subside and simply leave us with our primary objective reached and our physical and mental integrity intact. On the other hand, we fear for our lives and well-being, and evade alternative solutions that are beyond our willingness to pursue. We do both, and attain *neither* objective, because we merely change costumes without concomitant change in our behavior – the very behavior which got us into trouble in the first place. Despite the evidence to the contrary, we have on record the testimony of Henry Simmons, director of the FDA's Bureau of Drugs, who contended that DES cannot really be considered a carcinogen; rather, it is simply an estrogen that is safe under normal circumstances. Simmons' definition of "normal circumstances" may be somewhat less rigid than that of the rest of us, although FDA approval of DES as a "Morning After Pill" for emergency use only is no more informative. Some insight can be obtained from the package insert that accompanies DES, which specifies that a therapeutic abortion is strongly recommended if a woman finds that she was pregnant at the time DES was ingested. (DES is only "effective" within 72 hours following intercourse, in that it will only prevent implantation; once implantation has occurred, DES loses its antifertility properties.)

Arguments about the utility of DES have covered the gamut described above, and researchers continue to seek a more satisfactory solution, not necessarily through a ban on its use, but through the search for a better dosage of the drug – i.e., the recorded cases of vaginal and cervical cancer developed because the initial dosages of DES during the 1940s and 1950s were *too high.* It has been asked, "How little is enough?" Enough for what? To prevent conception? To prevent transplacental chemical carcinogenesis? To prevent miscarriage? To avoid an epidemic of cervical and vaginal cancer in adolescent girls? To make a cow grow to maturity faster? In this sense, *any* is too much. There are other means to accomplish our goals, means within our capacity to comprehend and implement if we would resort to other than ad hoc solutions. Ralph Nader's Health Research Group published a report on DES on December 8, 1972 which, among other facts, states the following:

1. As early as 1953, Dieckman published a study which cast serious doubt on the efficacy of DES in preventing a miscarriage. [*Am. J. Ob. Gyn. 66*] In a review of existing studies on this use in 1958, Goldzieher [*Am. J. Ob. Gyn.*, *75*, 1202] concluded that "there is no statistical evidence for the value of stilbestrol therapy."

Before Congress, FDA Commissioner Edwards was also unable to provide scientific evidence for the effectiveness of DES, but replied that there must be some "because of its widespread use in the medical profession."

2. Whether chloramphenicol for treating acne, penicillin for the common cold, or DES to prevent abortions the problem is much the same. Widespread use by the medical profession is very often widespread misuse.
3. The November 1971 FDA Drug Bulletin warning all physicians against use of DES if pregnant has, according to many obstetricians, significantly decreased its use to prevent miscarriages. Despite this, however, sales of DES for 1972 *increased* over 1971. Total DES sales for 1971 were $1,844,000 [price to the manufacturer]. Nine month figures for Lilly, the major supplier, [as it is for DES used in animal feed] were up 4 percent from last year.
4. Both Roy Hertz . . . and Dr. Mort Lipsett of the National Institutes of Health, experts in hormonal cancer, have repeatedly stated that the best available information suggests that all estrogens given in comparable doses and for comparable periods of time as DES would cause the same carcinogenic effects.

Dr. Hertz makes the following point:

5. "Addition of any artificial estrogen beyond the natural estrogen produced in the body disturbs a natural balance which, even under ideal natural conditions is precarious, demonstrated by the fact that one of each 16 women will develop breast cancer during her lifetime."

All synthetic estrogens, whether they be the commonly used oral anovulants or DES, are contraindicated in women having a family history of breast or genito-urinary cancer.

In an article appearing in *The Nation's Health* (June, 1973), the case is made that safety is an ephemeral concept, one of degree. "The Delaney Clause states that any residue of a known carcinogen, in any amount, cannot be tolerated, and DES, a synthetic hormonal compound, is covered by this definition." It is assumed that if the presence of a chemical causes certain effects on an animal, there are likely to be similar effects on humans. Absolute safety is neither called for nor possible.

Safety is a policy question . . . which demands the weighing of properly identified risks and benefits by the public. It is not an object of scientific determinism. The weighing mechanisms can be improved. The Delaney Clause, unlike any other section of the Food, Drug and Chemical Act, recognizes and is premised upon the limitations of science. Since science could never be sure of a chemical's safety, it seemed obvious [in banning the use of DES in cattle feed] that as a matter of policy we should be cautious in allowing the use of chemicals.

The article contends that "as a matter of practical necessity . . . we often regulate more out of fear of the unknown than out of respect and appreciation for the known." Finally, we are informed that the cattle industry is not worried about the ban on DES; a new drug compound — Synovex — consisting of estrogen benzoate and progesterone will soon replace DES. But Dr. Morton Lipsett of NIH has been quoted as saying, "Whatever dangers you want to attribute to DES you can attribute to Synovex." Another ad hoc approach, another clinical, legal, social, and regulatory battle — the same confusion all over again.

So we can conclude that DES is not really such a special case, after all. It is dramatic, in that its use is associated with death and one of mankind's most feared and terrible diseases. It is tragic, because it occurs in vulnerable young girls and women who had nothing to do with their predicament. It is controversial, because of the economic incentives operating against its removal from the pharmaceutical supermarket. But the problems it raises are in fact not unlike the problems associated with drug therapy in general; it is the wrong answer for the wrong question.

8

THE LAW AS A SYSTEM
OF CONTROL

Although considerable overlap exists when we approach discussions of law, regulation, and the ethics of experimentation with human subjects, it is conceptually possible to distinguish between certain components of each social strut. The role of law is viewed by some major spokespersons in the discourse to follow.

The Role of Law in Human Experimentation

I take the liberty of using experimentation and therapeutics interchangeably here, although there are no doubt semantic differences which various exceptions to my logic will obviate. The assumption that all therapeutics is experimental was made earlier, and I contend that the same legal ramifications apply to each dimension.

Calabresi (1969: 387-405) provides the perspective of the torts lawyer, and discusses the unresolved conflict between belief in the sanctity of life and our tendency to place some values (including the viability of future lives) above the life of the individual. He observes:

[C]onflict [between life and values] . . . suggests the need for a quite complex structuring to enable us *sometimes* to sacrifice lives, but hardly ever to do it blatantly and as a society, and above all to allow this sacrifice only under quite rigorous controls.

The question becomes one of the role of institutionalized law in furthering and protecting the various interests of society, and of the individuals and groups that comprise society.

I shall limit the argument at this point to the legal aspects of contraceptive medicine, although obviously many of the same principles apply in other domains of biomedical technological innovation and human experimentation. Dubuc (1968) believes that "there is no difference in principle, from the legal point, between oral contraceptives and other contraceptives." But the legal role must be large enough to encompass two aspects of the contraceptives: 1) the civil aspect; and 2) the penal aspect. The first aspect "deals with the regulation of [contraceptive] . . . sales and the civil responsibility of the doctor who prescribed them." The penal aspect "deals with the prohibition of some of its faces under the criminal code."

The civil aspect is fundamentally no different from other problems of civil law, in that oral anovulants are drugs as are any other ethical (prescription) drugs. Although Dubuc is writing from the standpoint of law in Quebec, Canada, our legal traditions stem from the same British foundations, and many of his points are comparable. He writes:

[In the area of civil law] It follows that the prescription of oral contraceptives, in the case where they should not be prescribed, could possibly engage the civil responsibility of the physician, if after effects result that could have been foreseen by the physician. Since the complete effectiveness of oral contraception has not been established, a physician who prescribed them could not be held responsible for an undesired pregnancy, unless he would have assured his patient that the results would be totally effective and in this case, the patient would have to prove that she had taken the contraceptives exactly as prescribed by the physician in order to avoid the pregnancy.

There is also the question of whether the physician is aware of the contraindications of oral anovulants, and his responsibility of informing the woman of the risk inherent in their use under specified medical conditions. If the prescribing physician were to fail to take the contraindications into account, or to inform his patient of the concomitant risks, he would, one would assume, be liable under civil law for malpractice.

Dubuc's views on the penal aspect will not be discussed, since they are based upon criminal statutes different from those existing in the United States. This aspect would include criminal violation of sales, prescription, and possession of certain drugs, not directly applicable to oral anovulants and their availability in the United States. Probably the penal aspect has had some applicability in the United States in cases where physicians have illegally sold oral anovulants to their patients, although the matter does not concern us for present purposes. Individual states in some cases have their own laws prohibiting the prescription of oral anovulants for contraceptive purposes (e.g., Massachusetts), and violations are reputed to be not uncommon, since oral anovulants *are* legal for *other* gynecological purposes (e.g., regulating menstrual periods), and the difficulties inherent in determining when a physician has prescribed the same compound for one purpose or another are overwhelming. (Thus we might be led to expect a high incidence of gynecologic problems requiring oral anovulant therapy in Massachusetts.)

The civil aspect is the most illuminating in the United States, I believe, and the arguments in this chapter largely reflect this viewpoint.

Paul, writing in the *Temple Law Quarterly* (1972), states:

Since 1965, when the first Pill case was litigated,* many lawsuits have been filed by women who claimed to have been harmed by the Pill. Most of these suits were settled out of court because drug companies sought to avoid both the possibility of a larger adverse judgement in court and bad publicity. Until 1971,** those cases that did reach the courts had all resulted in decisions for the defendant drug manufacturers. Plaintiffs simply had a difficult time convincing the courts that the Pill *could* cause harm.

All suits filed were against the manufacturers of ethical drugs, and this meant that they had secured FDA approval before marketing their drug. In order to be granted approval, the manufacturer must submit a formal application containing all relevant information concerning the drug's chemical structure, known side effects, contraindications, and other information about intended testing methodologies to be employed. The approval comes only after an FDA committee made up of physicians, chemists, and pharmacologists evaluates all of this informa-

---

*Simonait v. Searle, Circuit Court for Kent County, Grand Rapids, Michigan, Civil Case No. 1916, tried May 18–26, 1965.

**Tobin v. G.D. Searle, Inc., U.S. Dist. Ct. (S.D.N.Y.), 66 Civ. 3650, tried Mar. 15–Apr. 24, 1970: Meinert v. G.D. Searle, Inc., Supreme Ct., Kings County, N. Y., Case No. 2549-65, tried March 11-April 15, 1970.

tion on the New Drug Application (NDA) to ensure safety and efficacy. A judgment is made as to whether the drug can be used safely only under the supervision of a physician and, if it must be, it is designated an ethical drug. In this event, any labeling information that accompanies the drug is intended for use by the prescribing physician. "Once ethical drug firms have won necessary approval to permit sale, use and distribution of their product it will be hard to prove it unsafe."

The underlying philosophy is that the experimenting professions must develop their own controls and interpret the common law according to their own unique perspectives, objectives, and needs, supplementing the relevant legal principles with statutory and administrative controls (Calabresi, 1969: 409). This is intended to provide a comprehensive, integrated framework that looks out for the interests of all parties concerned. In reality, these functions and institutions frequently fail to complement or supplement one another, and appear to be at odds.

Dr. Walsh McDermott of Cornell University (Jaffe, 1969) denotes this situation as a "benign hypocrisy" whereby:

the *Helsinki Declaration,* the FDA regulations, and similar pronouncements are "honest reflections of our culture complete with all its hypocrisies" and to follow them "to the letter . . . would produce the curious situation in which the only stated public interest is that of the individual. The future interest of society and its sometime conflict with the interest of the individual, in effect, are ignored. . . ." It has been most unwise to try to extend the principle of "a government of laws not men" into areas of such great ethical subtlety as clinical investigation.

Calabresi (1969: 414), not in full agreement with McDermott, explains his position this way:

The generalization I would derive from this criticism is that the system of legal controls should be based for the most part not on detailed statutory or administrative rules applicable to all experiments, but on standards allowing leeway for the exercise of judgement, whether the instrumentality be the experimenter, a control committee, a funding organization, an administrative body, or a court.

Calabresi further argues that "judges are sensitive to the ethos of the times," and that we should:

proceed on the hypothesis, therefore, that in framing our ethical principles the common law will be hospitable to procedures that recognize the social value of human experimentation without sacrificing the interests of patients and subjects.

Advocacy on the Part of the Patient/Subject

I wish to make a few brief comments on the importance of advocacy in this, the area of law as a system of control. Adams (1973: 840-842) discusses the role of the social worker in relation to recent advances in biomedical technology, although the arguments are equally applicable to sociologists, physicians, lawyers, or demographers. Adams believes that it is up to us to defend one another — and ourselves — "when the human, moral, civil, and legal rights of [people] . . . are transgressed by individuals, groups, or social institutions." We must be sensitive to the following aspects of our responsibilities: 1) immediate versus future benefits; 2) preventative versus corrective action; 3) the common good versus the good of the individual; 4) and finally, the too ready subordination of "the less obvious human claims to the immediate exigencies of research."

The problem world-wide has been that the individual, the culture, has lacked an effective, sufficiently sensitive and powerful advocate when it has been attacked by chance or design either from outside (e.g., U.S. television programming in Latin America) or through its own organizational myopia. The courts offer *one* forum for debate and redress, but there remains the question of whether common law is the right place for these crucial responsibilities. Getting just a little ahead of my argument, I wish to quote Paul once again (1972: 499):

We should . . . take the Pill out of the legal arena since that is hardly the most effective place to settle problems of this nature. Litigation is expensive and troublesome for all concerned [manufacturer, doctor and consumer]. Differences in interpretation of the law, even within the same jurisdiction, will make Mrs. X a winner and Mrs. Y a loser on similar facts and circumstances. A more pragmatic solution has to be found.

If we do remove oral anovulants from the legal arena, then where should controversy properly be resolved? Regulatory agencies have been shown to defer to the courts, and citizens must argue their case in civil court, not on the steps of the Food and Drug Administration in Washington, D.C. The fact that "litigation is expensive and troublesome" has little relevance here; what kind of a rationale is implied by a statement of this nature in the legal literature? True, the law is often arbitrary and lacks consistency, but this is insufficient reason to leave other institutions with the responsibility of adjudication.

In an article entitled, "Laws Alone Can't Make Drugs Safe," Lawrence Lessing (*Fortune*, March, 1963) rightfully observes that new legislation will not necessarily protect the consumer from untoward effects. Neither, for that matter, will the strict application of laws already on the books. *What we are in fact doing is seeking the proper place to redress the evils and shortcomings of allopathic medicine.* And yet, Lessing contends (p. 123):

It is impossible to determine definitely whether a drug is free from harmful effects unless it is tried widely on humans – and that inevitably means risking lives.

Lessing is no doubt correct, although he is arguing in order to justify the use of humans for testing drugs under the allopathic approach to therapeutics. However, the argument goes much beyond the clinical setting, for we can readily see that the allopathic approach is just as frequently applied to societal problems: the allopathic solution to population growth, or the allopathic approach to alcoholism, or the allopathic solution to crime. The real solution lies in finding *alternative* ways of treating individuals and groups that do not have to mean risking lives, or peace of mind, or cultural derangement. Perhaps the role of the social scientist ought to be reconsidered in this light and he or she ought to assume the burdens of advocacy for society.

Lessing (pp. 124-125) fails to consider these alternatives, and offers us the following insight:

The best hope of reducing the risks is the continued improvement of scientific clinical testing or clinical pharmacology, a relatively new and far from fully developed branch of medicine. In the not remote past, drugs still came into use slowly by the historical trial-and-error method that sometimes produced disasters rivaling the thalidomide's, in horror if not in scope. As science began to penetrate medicine, less than a century ago, the development and initial testing of new drugs became the province of the individual scientific investigator of a disease, mainly in the universities, and most of the basic discoveries continue to come from this source.

Lessing informs us that over 400 new drug applications (NDAs) are filed each year, and approximately 90 percent of all prescriptions written today were unheard of fifteen years ago. *"Formerly the pharmaceutical industry made only what the doctor prescribed; now the doctor prescribes what the industry makes."* [Emphasis added.]

Lessing continues:

The sheer volume of new drugs, however, poses an immense problem in clinical testing. It is lessened somewhat by the fact that of the more than 400 new drugs each year perhaps only forty (10 percent) are entirely new chemical entities; the rest are new formulations, new dosage forms, or slight molecular modifications of existing products. *Since even the slightest change in a chemical compound often markedly alters its biological or therapeutic effect, the modifications must generally be tested with all the care of entirely new drugs.* [Emphasis added.]

Recall Sarason's argument that "those who create new settings always want to do something new, usually unaware that they are armed with, and will subsequently be disarmed by, categories of thought which help produce the conditions the new setting helps to remedy" (1972). Once again, medical and pharmaceutical innovation gives the appearance that reality has been altered, when in fact the changes are mere masquerades for social change. A new medicine, a new dosage, a new method of administering a drug – none of these bears the slightest relationship to the fundamental etiology of the problems being addressed.

Litigation

Litigation surrounding the use of oral anovulants and other ethical drugs is codified in the law under Theories of Liability. Recovery for damages against ethical drug manufacturers is predicated upon two theories of liability: 1) negligence and 2) strict liability (warranty and tort). A third theory of liability may be applicable in the event of a mass campaign in the areas of public health inoculation or population control; that is, the inversion of condemnation, where socialization of services such as the administration of polio vaccine results in harm to the consumer. Should the consumer suffer as a consequence of *being legally required* to avail him or herself of a preventative measure, that individual can theoretically recover for damages incurred. Schlesinger (1970: pp. 396-397) cites the Decision of the German Bundesgerichtshof of February 19, 1953, in which the plaintiff, who was vaccinated as a child pursuant to a compulsory vaccination statute, and suffered permanent injuries due to post-vaccinal encephalitis. The plaintiff sued the state, although she was unable to prove that the vaccination had been negligently performed, "on the theory that in submitting to the public duty created by the compulsory vaccination statute, she had been compelled to sacrifice her health in the public interest, and that for this loss she should receive adequate compensation from the community." The court ruled that it was unnecessary to prove negligence, and that "*A fortiori* ... the community owes compensation to one who was forced to make a special sacrifice — i.e., a sacrifice not exacted from other persons in the same class — involving loss of life or health." Without going any more deeply into the theory of inversion of condemnation, we can readily see the implications of this precedent if mass population control measures, particularly those involving pharmacotherapeutics or surgery, were to be instituted. Aware of the risks inherent in allopathic medicine, the state or some other entity such as an ethical drug manufacturer or a physician could conceivably be held liable under such a condition of therapeutics.

Paul (1972) notes that "the presence of a *duty* to warn is the *sine qua non* in an action for negligence against an ethical drug manufacturer." The duty to warn is based upon weighing the likelihood and severity of harm against the feasibility of giving a warning. While it can generally be said to be impossible for ethical drug manufacturers to warn against all possible injuries resulting from the use of their products, the complexity of modern chemical products has so increased the likelihood of harm to unsuspecting users that the duty to warn is being expanded in the law (Paul, 1972: 485-486). Since there is no duty to warn the consumer of known side effects or contraindications, provided that the prescribing physician and the medical profession are warned, manufacturers must be very judicious in wording their advertisements and warnings, since "ambiguities will be construed against the one who chooses the words used.'" This duty to warn carries with it responsibilities to inform the physician of new developments regarding the products, and even to warn a small group of idiosyncratic users about the potential hazards resulting from use of the drugs. Such information is usually conveyed to the physician by drug "detailmen," salesmen who represent the drug companies, although other sources include advertisements in medical journals, the *Physicians' Desk Reference* (PDR) published annually by the pharmaceutical industry, and a variety of brochures and literature sent out over the course of the drug's use. The detailmen, through their ready access to the physician, are the most informative and current form of notification, since the physician's time is so taken with other obligations that keeping abreast of every new change in wording and report that appears through the mails is too slow and time-consuming to be sufficiently effective. On the other hand, the drug detailmen do represent the pharmaceutical companies, and this bias no doubt distorts their advice and information when sales and profits are threatened; competition is very strong.

There is considerable debate over whether information about ethical drugs should also be provided the patient, given the increasing sophistication and knowledge of the general public. This has already led to at least one major lawsuit, reported in the *Ithaca Journal* (April 9, 1973), in which a $7 million action was filed against the Syntex Corporation by a Mrs. Laraine Henard, who suffered a stroke which she contends was due to one of Syntex's oral anovulants. Mr. and Mrs. Henard argued that the manufacturer failed to give adequate warnings about dangerous side effects, and that the pill taken, Norinyl 2, left her partially paralyzed. Mrs. Henard contended that she was influenced to take the drug by a booklet in her obstetrician's office entitled "The Pills and Human Happiness," which in its 64 pages failed to give any hint of possible trouble resulting from use of the drug. "The suit asks $1.75 million in general damages and $5.25 million in punitive damages. Defendants are Syntex; Mrs. Henard's obstetrician, Dr. Richard C. Wallace of Bakersfield; and a doctor who also prescribed the pills, Dr. Harry Wong."

The article points out:

The Henards' action is far from the first suit charging the pills with harmful side effects. And since 1966 the Food and Drug Administration has on occasion complained about misleading advertising by the makers of oral contraceptives. But attorneys say this is apparently the first suit accusing a pharmaceutical company of misleading or false advertising in material — such as the Syntex booklet — directed specifically at women themselves.

The case is currently in litigation, and the outcome should set a precedent for numerous other suits on behalf of individuals who have suffered due to related negligence.

Paul (1972) states that "manufacturer's strict liability developed when it became apparent that products could be produced, without negligence, which caused harm." The concept of risk allocation emerged when it became clear that the law required a position capable of dealing with situations "where there is no blame on either side . . . in view of the exigencies of social justice, who can best bear the loss and hence shift the loss by creating liability where there has been no fault." Strict liability subsumes both warranty and tort theories, although both are interdependent.

Under the theory of breach of implied warranty, it would be incumbent to show that the drug is unfit for a particular purpose or unmerchantable. However, FDA approval implies that the drug in question is both fit and merchantable, and contesting a drug under breach of implied warranty would be very difficult, given the nature of our regulatory statutes. Paul argues that plaintiffs have maintained that a drug like the oral anovulant, which is supposed to prevent pregnancy and to regulate the menstrual cycle, but which also causes harm, is neither fit for its intended purpose nor is it merchantable. "Lack of foreseeability on the part of the seller in discovering a flaw in his product does not bar liability for breach of implied warranty."

Under theory of strict liability in tort, a plaintiff must prove that a product was sold in a defective condition, unreasonably dangerous to the consumer; that the manufacturer was in the business of selling said product; and that the product reached the consumer without substantial change in the condition in which it was sold.

To date, there have been two major obstacles to recovery under a theory of strict liability: 1) Comment K of No. 402 A of the Restatement of Torts 2d; and 2) a lack of legal precedent. Comment K addresses products "which by their nature are unavoidably unsafe yet are deemed necessitous to society because of their remarkable qualities."

Comment K reveals that dangerous but useful products must be *properly prepared* and *marketed* and *users adequately warned* of untoward effects. Paul contends:

PREGNANCY AS A DISEASE

One never reaches the stage of balancing risks against benefits unless those criteria are first satisfied. Since inadequacy of warnings has been the basis for most suits against Pill manufacturers, Comment K would seem to have no application if such an allegation is proven.

Paul goes on to remark that even the oral anovulants produced with adequate warnings might not qualify for Comment K protection today:

As more harmful side effects and societal effects are discovered, Comment K would seem to have less efficacy than it did five years ago. *Moreover, unlike the Pasteur Process, there are safe viable alternatives to the Pill, and it is doubtful that having children can be equated at this time, to a "loathsome dreadful disease" like rabies.* [Emphasis added.]

On the other hand, pregnancy, we contend, has in fact been likened to a dread disease, and our medical, legal, and regulatory institutions have responded accordingly.

Because of wider judicial acceptance, theories of strict liability are more frequently being used today, but theories of negligence are included with strict liability counts "because the courts and judges are apt to regard substantial damages as more appropriate where evidence of actual carelessness is present" (Paul, 1972).

Morris and Moritz (1971) believe that, while most states have regulatory statutes covering contraceptive devices or information, they do not create any serious problem for the practicing physician. (It should be noted that physicians are being included as defendants along with pharmaceutical manufacturers in liability suits.) The statutes of Colorado, Delaware, Idaho, Indiana, Iowa, Minnesota, Nevada, New York, Ohio, Oregon, Wisconsin and Wyoming openly permit contraceptive advice from a physician. Those of Arizona, Arkansas, California, Kansas, Louisiana, Maine, Michigan, Mississippi, Missouri, Nebraska, New Jersey, North Carolina, Pennsylvania, and Washington permit physicians to give contraceptive advice if required for the health of the patient. Recently, the following states have either repealed anti-birth control legislation or enacted laws permitting birth control activities: Alaska, California, Colorado, Florida, Georgia, Illinois, Indiana, Iowa, Kansas, Massachusetts, Michigan, Minnesota, Nevada, New York, Ohio, and West Virginia (page 104).

Morris and Moritz believe:

In such a rapidly changing field, especially in view of its moral overtones, the reader concerned herewith should consult legal advice as to the current situation in his particular jurisdiction, although the modern trend is certainly liberal in favor of legality.

The 1965 decision of the Supreme Court of the United States overturning the Connecticut anti-birth control statutes "is considered by many as marking a turning point in the birth control movement."

The increasing liberalization of voluntary family planning and the abolition of abortion restrictions will no doubt result in a greater number of women (and men) being exposed to the risk of untoward effects from the currently marketed contraceptives, and more suits on behalf of harmed consumers can probably be expected. It is therefore imperative that our legal institutions and statutes reflect the needs seen in this anticipated expansion of demand, and the subtleties of the claims.

The Development of Drug Laws in the United States

We now turn to a special article by Dr. Joseph F. Sadusk, Jr. (*Annals of Internal Medicine*, October, 1966), in which the subject of drugs and the public safety is discussed. Much of the following discussion is based upon Dr. Sadusk's presentation.

The seminal piece of legislation in the United States food and drug laws was the Pure Food and Drugs Act of 1906. Although it marked a turning point for the pharmaceutical industry and the public interest, it had several flaws that had to be redressed by further legislative action on the part of Congress.

The first deficiency discovered was that the 1906 Act lacked adequate specification about jurisdiction over curative claims. The Sherley Amendments of 1912 were added in order to expand the meaning of the term "misbranded" to include false and fraudulent claims about therapeutic value. Because the government was unable to prove fraudulent interest, the Sherley Amendments lacked the requisite teeth, and were therefore unenforceable.

Some thirty years later, in the 1940s, it became apparent as more potent drugs were developed that much tighter control over public distribution was needed. In 1951, the Humphrey-Durham Amendment separated drugs into two classes: 1) ethical drugs to be administered only by a physician's prescription; and 2) patent, over-the-counter drugs that could be used safely with medical supervision. New categories of drugs continued to emerge during the 1950s, but not until the thalidomide tragedy of 1962 did the medical community fully appreciate the risks inherent in some of the newer formulations and chemicals. Thalidomide, a sedative sold without prescription in Europe, was never marketed in the United States because of a fluke when a woman employee of the FDA single-handedly prevented its approval for use in the United States by recalling a study of the possibility of the drug's teratogenic effects; the drug had been distributed in limited quantities in the United States for purposes of clinical investigation. The attention given the European thalidomide tragedy by the press created a burgeoning demand for more rigorous control of pharmaceuticals, and the Kefauver-Harris Drug Amendments of 1962 were rapidly enacted. These required the following measures on behalf of the public:

1. Both the safety and the efficacy of a drug had to be proven before it could be publicly marketed.

2. Necessary controls had to be established for the distribution and use of investigational drugs.

3. High quality had to be guaranteed in the manufacture of drugs.

4. Authoritative and swift mechanisms for the removal and for the approval of NDAs were instituted.

5. Continuous monitoring of drugs had to be conducted so that ineffective or dangerous drugs could be controlled or modified.

6. Ethical drug advertising was placed under review and control.

Finally, in 1965, the Drug Abuse Control Amendments were introduced, and went into effect on February 1, 1966. These amendments placed certain categories of drugs – such as amphetamines, barbiturates, and hallucinogens – under control of the appropriate government agency.

The elemental Food, Drug, and Cosmetic Act of 1938, in addition to other amendments up through 1965, now places the control of production, development, and use of these drugs under the auspices of the FDA.

Here, the scientific community, the pharmaceutical industry, and the Food and Drug Administration itself must develop a degree of expertise which was not dreamed of a decade ago. Organizational structures for such scientific and regulatory purposes are not accomplished in a year or two — the matter is so complex and properly qualified manpower are in such short supply that a half a decade or more will be needed to fully implement the law.

Lasagna, in his fascinating volume, *The Doctor's Dilemmas* (1962: 201-202), quotes Harvard's Henry Beecher, who writes:

It is not my view that many rules can be laid down to cover experimentation in man. . . . Rules are not going to curb the unscrupulous. Such abuses as have occurred are usually due to ignorance and inexperience. . . . Eventually, the broad gap between the law of the land and its interpretation, on the one hand, and scientifically, ethically, and morally sanctioned experimentation in man, on the other hand, must be narrowed, if not closed. This legal development can be helpful and directed toward progress or can be harmfully restrictive. Which it shall be will be determined by the breadth of understanding expended on this complex subject.

The law may not be able to prevent or correct all the sociocultural injustices committed on our own people or on others, but it provides an excellent setting for informed discussion and logical decision-making, taking into account historical forces and contemporary views of the world. Fears have been voiced, largely by the medical profession (*British Medical Journal,* 1971; *Journal of the American Medical Association,* 1970; Sadusk, 1966; *The Lancet,* 1971) that outside control by the legal or regulatory institutions would constitute an undesirable intrusion on the doctor-patient relationship, and the autonomy that a physician requires to practice allopathic medicine. It would, certainly, be an intrusion, although I would not necessarily connote the intrusion as undesirable. The tasks are too important, and the lives of people are too precious, for us to continue to place our destinies in the hands of a few who, however well-meaning they may be, are trained primarily in biological, allopathic approaches to human problems that often lie outside the domain of the clinician's expertise. There is room for a great variety of input here, and our ultimate survival as a sociocultural system may depend upon our willingness to maintain a pool of alternatives in the face of constantly changing environmental demands. What has not worked might well be abandoned, what appears to threaten our well-being might best be conditioned by what we know, and new approaches to social problems and pathology ought to be sought and welcomed. The law can serve as a repository for our changing perspectives on the sanctity of human life, on the benevolence or malevolence of our professional agents, and the perpetuation of control over our environments as new technological innovations are developed and implemented.

The Lancet (March 13, 1971: 533-534) writes of the relation between doctors and outside organizations:

. . . established to satisfy the demands of people who find that the medical profession does not fully meet their needs.

Increasingly often it is the patients who call [or seek to call] the tune — for example in seeking contraception, abortion, cosmetic operations, or simply inoculations to protect them against disease in foreign travel. Many doctors resent such calls on their time, because they may seem to undermine clinical authority, on moral grounds, or because such work is mostly tedious and repetitive. For these largely "non-consultative" needs, people come to doctors not so much as patients seeking expert advice as clients bent on specific aid.

. . . the present-day citizen, maturing earlier and more knowledgeable than his parents, knows what he wants and is intent on getting it. If, in his role as client, he receives a cold welcome from his doctor, he will turn elsewhere: and agencies, each set up to meet one particular need, will proliferate.

Drug Litigation of Special Significance

Since 1960, the number of lawsuits filed against oral anovulant manufacturers has continued to increase, with particular attention being given to the issues of negligence, tort, and related legal theories on which the cases are predicated. This brief section will discuss some of the more interesting and informative lawsuits that have occurred during the past decade.

Curran (*The New England Journal of Medicine* 285, 19: November 4, 1971) writes of "The Birth of a Healthy Child Due to Negligent Failure of 'Pill': Benefit or Loss?", describing a case where the husband and wife brought suit against a pharmacist who mistakenly filled a prescription for an oral anovulant with a tranquilizer. The mother, who already had seven children, took the "pill" faithfully, became pregnant, and subsequently gave birth to an unwanted, eighth, healthy baby. The parents sued: 1) to recover the costs of rearing an eighth child; 2) for compensation for the pain and anxiety of pregnancy and childbirth; 3) for medical and hospital expenses; and 4) for the wife's loss of wages due to pregnancy, childbirth, and child-rearing.

When the case came to trial, the parents had to rely on precedent, which minimized the likelihood of recovery, at least for help in raising a healthy child. A precedent had been set for "wrongful life" on the part of the child himself rather than the parents, and had alleged damages owing to the pain and stigma of illegitimacy.

However, this case (Troppi vs. Scarf) was unusual in that the Michigan Court of Appeals reversed the ruling of the lower court and held all four bases of recovery valid and actionable under Michigan law. A jury will now decide the assessment of damages, if the allegations are held to be true.

Clear negligence was shown on the pharmacist's part. Under the law, pharmacists owe a very high degree of duty in filling a prescription, and this duty was violated here. The pharmacist is liable for the harm done.

The pharmacist-defendant argued that the parents had a legal obligation to mitigate the damages, since the negligence was actionable by law, by having an abortion or by putting the child up for adoption. In reply, after much deliberation, the court asserted:

"The [pharmacist] does not have the right to insist that the victim of his negligence have the emotional and mental makeup of a woman who is willing to abort or place a child for adoption."

The court ruled as a matter of law that no mother, wed or unwed, can reasonably be required to abort [even if legal] or place her child for adoption.

Curran observes that recently courts have applied what is called "social engineering" to torts and have rendered very large verdicts for more indirect and less measurable "losses" such as pain, mental anguish, and loss of reputation. Courts have also found many more such losses actionable, and physicians have now become aware of how they may be called to answer for negligence in medical malpractice suits. As a result, one insurance company covering approximately 18,000 physicians suggested that they obtain signed statements from patients before prescribing oral anovulants, specifying that they had been informed of the inherent risks associated with these drugs. *The Journal of the Kansas Medical Society* (72: January, 1971) suggests:

> The burden of damages for side-effects should fall on the manufacturer as a cost of production . . . and this should prompt more ambitious testing and research, which may ultimately result in a convenient, effective, and safe oral contraceptive.

The idea is appealing, although we still have not managed to get away from the concept of a new and better drug; responsibility is simply shifted and routinized.

Sandra Blair, in the *Hastings Law Journal* (1972), argues:

> The use of birth control pills can be seen as an uncontrolled experiment with disastrous consequences for some of its participants. Because of ineffective warnings to the user, many women unknowingly risk death or serious injury to prevent conception. Drug manufacturers must accept legal responsibility for the occasional disastrous consequences of this experiment.

Again, would simply controlling this massive experiment be sufficient to accomplish what we hope for — that is, the protection of the woman's health and physical integrity, the avoidance of pregnancy, and the lowering of society's growth rate? Would placing responsibility for damages on the manufacturers do this? No alternatives have been recommended or implied. We continue to search for ad hoc solutions that are not really solutions at all. To require more adequate warning, more precise wording in reports, more thorough clinical and laboratory testing, the assessment of severe penalties on violators of legal and regulatory statutes are no answers, except perhaps in the short run of events. People will continue to ingest drugs in the hope that their problems will somehow diminish or go away, side effects will continue to occur, and the same hackneyed arguments over who is responsible will continue. The conclusion that ". . . it is now irrefutable that the Pill does have the *propensity* for causing various types of harm to *some* people in *some* cases" (Paul, 1972: 492) tells us nothing that we do not already know, and is a long way from suggesting alternatives for correcting this state of affairs. Would a more detailed warning about the seriousness of side effects accompanying a package of oral anovulants do any better?

Paul (1972: 498) comes a little closer to the mark when he contends "In assessing what posture the law and society should take toward the Pill in the future we must first destroy the myth that the Pill in its present form is indispensable to society. At present there are at least seven other recommended methods of birth control with two being almost as effective."

Coccia (1968: 528) points out that we are dealing here with a nationwide industry involving only a proportion of the entire population. Each case must be studied on its own merits before we can append the appropriate law:

In ascendency in recent years has been the "center of gravity" or "dominant contacts" theory. Here, the court must review the case from the standpoint of determining which jurisdiction is so intimately involved with the issues at hand as to render their law appropriate to a determination of the issues.

Here we are searching for the proper geographic and legal setting for adjudication of legal issues pursuant to injustices allegedly suffered because of the oral anovulant mode of therapeutic intervention. The lack of consistency is apparent when we review the law literature recounting the major cases involving oral contraceptives (Coccia, 1968; Paul, 1972; Barrett, 1970; Blair, 1972; Noel, 1969; Dubuc, 1968). I contend that this search will continue until we develop a more encompassing policy with respect to allopathic medicine and the ethics of experimentation using human subjects. Until we do, few will wish to accept responsibility because they will not pretend to be capable of providing answers to the wrong questions.

The legal literature does not illuminate the real issues any better than does the demographic or clinical literature. In reworking the common law so as to accommodate better litigation on oral anovulants, we witness improvements in the structure of the law and consideration for the sanctity of human life, but this does not imply a concomitant improvement in the etiology of the problems that led to the litigation in the first place. Perhaps there is some feedback whereby the law will reflect and condition social behavior to a greater extent than it has in the past; much of the law has been archaic, and of little use in reformulating social and public policy. The law can provide *guidelines,* but it is we who must ultimately act and decide what we hope to accomplish, and the best means of going about it. Simply having more precise guidelines is not sufficient to bring about needed social reforms; we must want to try to do something different.

The Problem of Proof

Because of the intrinsic difficulties in establishing causality, the problem of proof in the legal arena is a controversial point that invariably works against the plaintiff. Since it is almost impossible to say with certainty that a particular drug is the direct cause of an untoward effect, given the variety of other events occurring to an individual while he or she is on the prescribed medication, proof is often determined through consensus or expert opinion. The plaintiff frequently finds him or herself in the position of needing one physician to testify against another physician in the event of malpractice litigation — an awkward situation, at best. In Pennsylvania, for example, litigation involving oral anovulants requires expert testimony from a physician specifying *unequivocally* that the oral anovulant caused the harm that is alleged. This absolute is, certainly, rarely obtained. Sadusk (1966: 853-854) informs us:

the establishment of a cause-effect relationship between drug and alleged reaction may be extremely difficult. This is because adverse reactions are generally nothing more or less than disease conditions . . . which may appear in an individual with or without the use of a drug.

If a plaintiff involved in a lawsuit over alleged harm caused by oral anovulants smokes, takes other medication, consumes alcohol, or has been involved in an automobile collision, her claims will be received in the court with some suspicion, especially when the court is not sensitive to the complexity of the evidence regarding thromboembolic phenomena and the use of these drugs. The question remains, when dealing with the concept of risk and probability, what does a jury do with the data in Table 10, based on British studies during the late 1960s? We must recall that in product liability cases, the plaintiff is responsible for proving that a defect in the product existed before it left the manufacturer and that the defect was the proximate cause of the alleged harm. Regardless of whichever theory of liability is argued, the "defect" would in any case be the result of inadequate warning. Problems of proof have been divided into two main classes: 1) proving that a defect exists in the product; and 2) determining that there is in fact a causal connection between the defect and the plaintiff's harm. To prove

TABLE 10

Thromboembolic Disease and The Oral Anovulants

	Death Rates		Hospitalization
	Age 20-34	Age 35-44	Age 20-44
Pill Users	1.5/100,000	3.9/100,000	47/100,000
Nonusers	0.2/100,000	0.5/100,000	5/100,000

Source: Joyce Barrett, "Product Liability and the Pill," 19 *Cleveland State Law Review* 3 (September, 1970: 475).

the first point, evidence has to be offered regarding the drug's physical and chemical properties that require warnings to the consumer (or indirect consumer, such as the patient); oral anovulants are difficult in this case, since such evidence is really incapable of proving that the drug caused the alleged harm (usually thromboembolic disease) — rather, "'it goes to the more threshold question of whether what was in it could do it '" (Paul, 1972: 490).

In any event, Paul contends (p. 493):

The burden of proof weights heavily in the manufacturer's favor on this issue at *this* time because the FDA did not order that the warnings on Pill inserts be changed until 1968 and 1969 and in most cases being litigated *now* the harm occurred *prior* to these revisions.

In proving causation the only evidence of any real probative value will be the testimony from medical experts, as knowledge of origin, causation and aggravation of specific diseases, like thrombophlebitis, lies in "scientific fields wherein the average juror or layman does not possess the knowledge or information from which to draw his own conclusions and must be guided by the opinions of experts who have acquired information on the subject."

Under normal circumstances competent experts are hard to find but in oral contraceptive cases the problem is much more acute because until recently, medical literature was ambivalent at best and medical opinion on the Pill frequently is colored by religious, moral and societal considerations.

When diseases such as thrombophlebitis are idiopathic (that is, self-originating), the problem of establishing proof is exacerbated, because certain predisposing conditions such as pregnancy and obesity confound the suspected potential effects of oral anovulants; the best that judges and juries have to go by is evidence of expert witnesses, plus literature that provides little more than statistically significant relationships.

Another problem in establishing causality is that of the intervening role of the prescribing physician. In finding negligence on the part of the physician, questions arise regarding the sufficiency of the manufacturer's warnings to the medical profession, as well as the thoroughness of the physician's insight into contraindications and the patient's idiosyncratic medical status:

If the doctor be adequately warned of all the hazards and *then* fails to exercise good judgement in prescibing the Pill or fails to secure an informed consent, he might be liable in an action for malpractice. (Paul, 1972: 496)

Certainly, adequate follow-up of the patient is crucial, although the frequency and adequacy of such continuous monitoring is questionable, given the demands on the physician's time and his knowledge of new findings and contraindications.

Is litigation to be viewed as a stopgap, inadequate means of regulating the contraceptive industry and the medical profession, once a population policy or non-policy is determined for the people of the United States? Or is it a continuous monitor of both public interest and changes in social attitudes toward therapeutic intervention and the sanctity of human and socio-cultural viability? Oral anovulants seem to have been born out of a concern for rapid demographic growth, and a search for short-cut, technological solutions to such social problems as poverty, inequitable income distribution, and the inability of certain social strata to rise from the lower levels of the stratification hierarchy.

What does this discussion recommend on the basis of current knowledge and future policy? Paul (1972: 500) contends:

If in the future, the FDA and drug manufacturers become aware of new and more serious side effects [which is the most likely possibility], then the product should be taken off the market until such time as it is made safe for public use.

I suspect that we already know enough about oral anovulants to justify removing them from the market, in that they have been shown to be sufficiently harmful — despite their efficacy — and that numerous alternatives are readily available and can be encouraged and used safely and effectively. Removal of oral anovulants from the market is not tantamount to threatening the public with burgeoning population growth, nor is it equivalent to increasing the incidence of maternal deaths due to unwanted pregnancy. Comparing the risk of death or disability from oral anovulants with that of pregnancy is simply illogical, given the state of other, relatively innocuous forms of contraception already marketed.

The role of the law is counterposed with the role of the regulatory agencies in the following chapter.

9

THE ROLE OF REGULATION

What we have been discussing is really the structure and process of our system's checks and balances in the realm of therapeutic intervention.

Southwick (*Science*, 1969, 1970: 1188-1189) states that since the Kefauver-Harris Drug Act was passed in 1962 in response to the thalidomide tragedy in some European countries, the FDA has been responsible for securing the safety and effectiveness of more than 7100 drugs that were already on the market, in addition to the 400 new drugs that enter the market each year.

The FDA has come under continuous fire from the drug industry, the medical profession, and the public, with criticism ranging from the contention that the FDA moves too slowly to that it moves too fast. Perhaps this is inevitable for a regulatory agency that is so badly understaffed, so short of resources, and entrusted with such a monumental task. In response, the FDA has gone through numerous structural, procedural, and personnel changes (three commissioners in four years). The FDA has been described as dealing not with "hard science but the making of decisions on the basis of hypotheses, without the evidence required by law."

Another criticism stems from the procedures of the FDA in approving and monitoring an NDA, and it is argued that the FDA's hands are tied because it cannot invoke an action to remove a particular drug from the market simply because that drug is shown to be ineffective. The other side argues that an ineffective drug is potentially hazardous: "Apparently people have to be dropping like flies all over the country before the FDA will employ the imminent hazard procedure."

Operating under a restrictive budget that appears at present to lack any likelihood of significant increase, the FDA, under its current Commissioner Charles O. Edwards, is doing its best to improve the efficiency of the FDA while simultaneously placating the attacks from Congress and the pharmaceutical industry. The public must also be convinced that the FDA is not addressing itself to the demands of the drug industry at the expense of the public interest. Future efforts continue to be directed toward improving the methodologies and understandings necessary to minimize the dangers of toxic drugs in the long run, but the FDA is established to deal with problems resulting from our society's insistence on allopathic solutions to problems. By definition, it is entrusted with perpetuating the allopathic approach to therapeutics, while at the same time ensuring the safety and efficacy of our drug armamentarium. This appears to be a losing battle – a situation where, periodically, the efforts of the FDA cause us all "to win the battle, but to lose the war." They, too, are asking the wrong questions. At best, not unlike the legal institutions, we can expect them to provide guidelines instrumental in facilitating ad hoc solutions to pervasive and complex social and medical problems.

The FDA employs the epidemiological approach, or "techniques ... [needed] for finding out *who* gets *what* and *why*" (Hill, 1971: 197-202). Hill believes that prevention is the ultimate goal of such procedures, and "under the heading of illness we can, and should, include all the departures from health [remaining undefined] from which man suffers whatever the cause." He continues:

Whether it be trauma, bacteria or virus, the environment and so on, some of the ills that we must consider today flow from our attempts to cure disease [or prevent ovulation, suggested to be the same thing] – by means of drugs – and from our attempts to prevent disease by means of vaccines.
... [The British Committee on the Safety of Drugs] seeks to detect the facts of causation so that [they] can see exactly how to prevent. ... we have to seek to prevent *ab initio* and then, as a secondary but vital part of our work, seek to detect where and how we have failed. So, in a sense, prevention comes first. ...

The only certain guarantee against adverse drug reactions is to do away with all drugs; Hill notes, "The final test of safety must always lie in the use of a drug in man ... *But if the public, or its representatives in high places, demand that all new treatments must be proved to be wholly without hazard, before use, then they are likely to end up with treatments without efficacy."* [Emphasis added.]

Schmeck (*The New York Times:* May 10, 1973) argues that a dangerous loophole in FDA guidelines permits new drugs to be used in clinical tests in human beings before adequate "acute, subacute and chronic animal toxicity tests" have been performed. The question remains: Such tests are not — could they ever be — sufficient? Schmeck believes:

> On the general issue, . . . the agency's current requirements for human experimentation are the most stringent in the world and are serving increasingly as models for other nations. . . . no system of animal testing could guarantee absolute safety for any drug. . . .

Lasagna (1962a: 183) adds to our comprehension of the complexity of FDA regulation:

> And even a change in the law will do nothing about the subtle and potentially most dangerous aspect of the FDA setup: the well-traveled two-way street between industry and Washington. Men from the drug industry have gone on to FDA jobs and — more important — FDA specialists have gone on to lucrative executive jobs in industry.

As long as such rapport exists between the FDA and the industry it is entrusted with censoring, the likelihood of biased and inadequate policy and action is enhanced.

Ideally, it can be said that the FDA, the pharmaceutical industry, the medical profession, the Congress, and the public are united in a common effort to protect and preserve the lives and well-being of American citizens.

Shifting responsibility for the monitoring and use of drugs does nothing to mitigate the problems of clinical and social toxicity addressed earlier. What is needed is an entirely new framework for the objectives of the public interest: I suspect that we need to depart from our total dependence on allopathic solutions to our societal problems, and that reorganization and new guidelines that have been implemented to date have not been relevant to creating new settings and a future society less dependent upon what has failed in the past.

10

SUMMARY AND DISCUSSION

Scope of the Study

My intention has been to present an alternative medical paradigm which is more attuned to the reality of therapeutic pharmacology in contemporary society. The overriding objective of technological intervention is control of the environment, but control effected otherwise than at the expense of social and individual well-being. *To do otherwise would amount to cultural aggression against those people who have become dependent upon medical professionals for solving what are basically social – not medical – problems.* When pregnancy is defined as a disease, traditional allopathic medicine poses exactly such a threat.

The scope of this study is broad, encompassing the ideologies of physicians, the pharmaceutical industry, the courts, watchdog agencies, and those concerned with the ethics of experimentation using human subjects. These are complex disciplines, and areas that they share in common are especially nebulous. The double bind is an ever-present threat when we counterpose issues of clinical efficacy, informed consent, drug safety, therapeutics and experimentation, and short- versus long-term effects.

The literature of these disciplines was examined with regard to implied concern for reinforcing the paradigm of pregnancy as a disease. An attempt was made to deduce the parameters of social toxicity which such a view of humanity suggests. Further discussion and generalization should not be confined to immediate, observable effects of therapeutic intervention, but should consider the way effects may reverberate through a socio-cultural system in generations to come. Demographic, social, and medical interventions are not linear; each deviation is likely to amplify itself in areas seemingly unrelated to the "initial kick." When these interventions are irreversible, we must be cautious indeed.

Does this mean to imply that the effects of oral anovulants are irreversible? Certainly, a woman can stop taking them at will. But once ingested, where do these extremely powerful steroidal hormones go? Are they simply and completely excreted from the body? Are they partially incorporated into the woman's tissues, genes, or psyche? *Are they passed on to future generations in a manner we cannot presently anticipate?* We do know that certain microstructural changes occur in the liver, kidneys, and blood of every woman who uses these drugs. They help to foster unnecessary dependence on "experts" who by training are taught to regard "patients" as clinical material isolated from their societal setting. *What else do they do?*

BIBLIOGRAPHY

Adams, M. "Science, Technology, and Some Dilemmas of Advocacy."
   Science 180 (May 25, 1973).
Alessandro Dall'Olio, P. "On the Use of Antiovulatory Drugs." *Riv.
   Ostet. Ginec.* 20 (March, 1965).
Allingham, J.D. "The End of Rapid Increase in the Use of Oral Anovu-
   lants? Some Problems in the Interpretation of Time Series of Oral
   Use Among Married Women." *Demography* 7, 1 (February, 1970).
Allingham, J.D., Balakrishnan, T.R. and Kantner, J.F. "Time Series of
   Growth in Use of Oral Contraception and the Differential Diffusion
   of Oral Anovulants." *Population Studies* 23 (1969): 43-51.
Barber, B., Lally, J.J., Makarushka, J.L. and Sullivan, D. *Research on
   Human Subjects — Problems of Social Control in Medical Experi-
   mentation.* New York: Russell Sage Foundation, 1973.
Barrett, Joyce. "Legal Risks in Selling or Prescribing 'The Pill'." *Journal
   of the Kansas Medical Society* 72 (January, 1971).
———. "Product Liability and the Pill." *Cleveland State Law Review*
   19, 3 (September, 1970):468.
Bateson, G. *Steps to an Ecology of Mind.* New York: Ballantine Books,
   1972.
Becker, W. "Cooperation of General Practitioners in Birth Control,
   Legal Questions about Prescription of the 'Pill'." *Ther Gegenw* 109
   (March, 1970).
Behrman, S.J., M.D. et al. *Fertility and Family Planning.* Ann Arbor:
   The University of Michigan Press, 1970.
Berliner, B. "'After' Pill Use Warned." *Syracuse Herald-American* (Feb-
   ruary 26, 1973).
Bernard, H.R. and Pelto, P.J. (eds.). *Technology and Social Change.*
   New York: The Macmillan Co., 1972.
Blair, Sandra. "Liability of Birth Control Pill Manufacturers," *Hastings
   Law Journal* 23 (May, 1972): 1526-1548.
Blumgart, Herrman L. "The Medical Framework for Viewing the Prob-

lem of Human Experimentation," *Ethical Aspects of Experimentation with Human Subjects, Daedalus* (Spring, 1969): 248-273.

Boston Women's Health Cooperative. *Our Bodies, Ourselves.* New York: Simon and Schuster, 1973. (See especially pages 111-120.)

Bracken, M.B. and Kasl, S.V. "Factors Associated with Dropping Out of Family Planning Clinics in Jamaica." *American Journal of Public Health* 63, 3 (1973).

Brinkmann, C.R., III. "The Pill Doesn't Poison." *Science* 164 (April 4, 1969).

British Medical Journal. "Stilboestrol and Cancer." *British Medical Journal* (Sept. 11, 1971).

Brody, J.E. "The Birth Pill Dispute." *The New York Times* (February 13, 1973).

———. "Pressure Grows for U.S. Rules on Intra-uterine Devices." *The New York Times* (June 4, 1973).

Cahn, E. "Drug Experiments and the Public Conscience," in P. Talalay (ed.) *Drugs in Our Society.* Baltimore, Maryland: The Johns Hopkins Press, 1964.

Calabresi, G. "Reflections on Medical Experimentation in Humans." *Daedalus* (Spring, 1969).

Carpenter, E. *Oh, What a Blow that Phantom Gave Me.* New York: Holt, Rinehart and Winston, 1972.

Cavers, D.F. "The Legal Control of the Clinical Investigation of Drugs: Some Political, Economic, and Social Questions." *Daedalus* (Spring, 1969).

Coccia, Michel A. "Manufacturer's Liability for Oral Contraceptives." *A.B.A. Sect. Ins. N. & C.L.* 512 (1968).

Commoner, B. *The Closing Circle, Nature, Man and Technology.* New York: Bantam Books, 1972.

Connell, E.B. "Effect of Washington Hearings on Contraceptive Use." *Delaware Medical Journal* 42 (August, 1970).

Connor, J.T. "The Functions of the Pharmaceutical Industry in Our Society," in P. Talalay (ed.) *Drugs in Our Society.* Baltimore, Maryland: The Johns Hopkins Press, 1964.

Cooper, M.H. *Prices and Profits in the Pharmaceutical Industry.* Oxford: Pergamon Press, 1966.

———. "Governmental Regulations of the Use of Human Subjects in Medical Research: The Approach of Two Federal Agencies." *Daedalus* (Spring, 1969).

———. "Legal Codes in Scientific Research Involving Human Subjects." *Lex et Scientia* 3 (April-June, 1966).

Curran, W.J. "Birth of a Healthy Child Due to Negligent Failure of 'Pill': Benefit or Loss?" *New England Journal of Medicine* 285, 19 (November 4, 1971).

Cutler, L.N. "Practical Aspects of Drug Legislation," in P. Talalay (ed.) *Drugs in Our Society.* Baltimore, Maryland: The Johns Hopkins Press, 1964.

Davis, K. "Social Demography," in B. Berelson (ed.) *The Behavioral Sciences Today.* New York: Harper Torchbook Edition, 1964.

Department of Health, Education, and Welfare. *The Institutional Guide* to *DHEW Policy on Protection of Human Subjects.* DHEW Publication No. (NIH) 72-102 (December 1, 1971). Public Health Service, National Institute of Health, Washington, D.C. 20402.

Duffy, B.J., Jr., M.D. and Wallace, Sister M.J. *Biological and Medical Aspects of Contraception.* Notre Dame: University of Notre Dame Press, 1969.

Dickey, R.P. and Dorr, C.H. "Oral Contraceptives: Selection of the Proper Pill." *Obstetrics and Gynecology* 33 (1969).

Diggory, P. "The Committee and the Pill." *Lancet* 1 (January 10, 1970).

Dowd, D.W. (ed.) *Medical, Moral and Legal Implications of Recent Medical Advances.* New York: Da Capo Press, 1971.

Dubos, R. *Mirage of Health.* New York: Harper, 1959.

―――. "On the Present Limitations of Drug Research," in P. Talalay (ed.) *Drugs in Our Society.* Baltimore, Maryland: The Johns Hopkins Press, 1964.

Dubuc, D. "Judicial Aspect of Contraceptive Drugs." *Laval Med* 39 (May, 1968).

Dukes, M.N.G. (ed.). *Social and Medical Aspects of Oral Contraception.* Amsterdam: Excerpta Medica Foundation: May, 1966.

Editorial. "Assessing the Risk." *Economist* 223 (April 8, 1967).

Editorial. "A Case of Confidence." *British Medical Journal* 1 (March 20, 1971).

Editorial. "Non-Medical Birth Control – A Neglected and Promising Field." *American Journal of Public Health* 63, 6 (June, 1973).

Editorial. "The Pill Controversy." *Southern Medical Journal* 63 (May, 1970): 608-610.

Editorial. "Products Liability and the Pill." 19 *Clev. St. L. R.* 468 (1970).

Editorial. "Stilboestrol and Cancer." *British Medical Journal* (September 11, 1971.)

Editorial. "Which Contraceptive?" *British Medical Journal* II (1963).

Ellul, J. *The Technological Society.* New York: Vintage Books, 1964.

Etzioni, A. "Healthcare and Self-Care: The Genetic Fix." *Society* 10, 6 (September/October, 1973).

Etzioni, A. and Remp, R. "Technological 'Short-Cuts' to Social Change." *Science* 175 (January 7, 1972).

―――. *Technological Shortcuts to Social Change.* New York: Russell Sage Foundation, 1973.

Family Planning Digest. "MDs Assume Poor Can't Remember to Take Pill." *Family Planning Digest* 1, 1 (January, 1972).

―――. "Poor Women Good Pill Users, Study Finds." *Family Planning Digest* 1, 1 (January, 1972).

―――. "New Findings: Liver, Libido, Breasts, Vitamin A." *Family Planning Digest* 1, 2 (March, 1972).

―――. "Clinics Teach Less than Patients Learn." *Family Planning Digest* 1, 2 (March, 1972).

―――. "Side Effects and Problems in Clinics Found Major Reasons for Dropouts." *Family Planning Digest* 1, 3 (May, 1972).

―――. "Find Orals Remain Acceptable, Useful." *Family Planning Digest* 1, 4 (July, 1972).

————. "Half of Estrogen Dose Prevents Pregnancy." *Family Planning Digest* 1, 5 (September, 1972).

————. "Ethics of Human Experimentation." *Family Planning Digest* 1, 5 (September, 1972).

————. "Pill and IUD Young Couples' First Choice." *Family Planning Digest* 1, 6 (November, 1972).

————. "British, U.S. Studies Find No Link Between Pill Use and Breast or Cervical Cancer." *Family Planning Digest* 2, 1 (January, 1973).

————. "Bleeding, Pregnancy Problems Found in Five Minipills Tested." *Family Planning Digest* 2, 1 (January, 1973).

————. "Acceptance of Risk by Patient Said to be 'Essence' of Informed Consent for Research." *Family Planning Digest* 2, 1 (January, 1973).

————. "Pill-Related Deaths: Are they Declining?" *Family Planning Digest* 2, 2 (March, 1973).

Feldman, J.G., Ogra, S., Lippes, J. and Sultz, H. "Patterns and Purposes of Oral Contraceptive Use by Economic Status." *American Journal of Public Health* 61 (1971).

Fertility and Sterility. "DES." *Fertility and Sterility* 1 (1960).

Fishbein, M. "Medical Progress in 1963." *Postgrad. Medicine* 35 (January, 1964).

Folkman, J. "Transplacental Carcinogenesis by Stilbestrol." *The New England Journal of Medicine* 285, 7 (August 12, 1971).

Ford, T.R. and DeJong, G.F. (eds.) *Social Demography.* Englewood Cliffs, New Jersey: Prentice-Hall, Inc., 1970.

Freund, Paul A. (ed.) *Experimentation with Human Subjects.* New York: George Braziller, 1970.

Gaddum, J.H. "A Perspective on Pharmacology," in P. Talalay (ed.) *Drugs in Our Society.* Baltimore, Maryland: The Johns Hopkins Press, 1964.

Galbraith, J.K. *The New Industrial State.* New York: New American Library, 1967.

Gambrell, R.D., Jr. "Immediate Postpartum Oral Contraception." *Obstetrics and Gynecology* 36, 1 (July, 1970).

Garai, P.R. "Advertising and Promotion of Drugs," in P. Talalay (ed.) *Drugs in Our Society.* Baltimore, Maryland: The Johns Hopkins Press, 1964.

Garcia, C.R. and Wallach, E. "Biochemical Changes and Implications Following Long-Term Use of Oral Contraception," in S.J. Behrman, M.D., et al. (eds.) *Fertility and Family Planning.* Ann Arbor: The University of Michigan Press, 1970.

Garfinkel, H. "Remarks on Ethnomethodology," in J.L. Gumperz and D. Hymes (eds.) *Directions in Sociolinguistics — The Ethnography of Communication.* New York: Holt, Rinehart & Winston, Inc., 1972.

Garland, J. "Dissemination of Information on Drugs to the Physician," in P. Talalay (ed.) *Drugs in Our Society.* Baltimore, Maryland: The Johns Hopkins Press, 1964.

Gerrard, E.A. President's Address. "Then and Now." *British Medical Journal* 5403 (July 25, 1964).

BIBLIOGRAPHY

Goldberg, D.C. "Demulen – Hastily Approved Drug." *Science* 170 (October 30, 1970).

Goldfarb, C. "DES – The Morning-After Pill." Statement of the Central New York Public Interest Research Group, Syracuse, New York (February 8, 1973).

Goldzieher, J.W. et al. "A Placebo-Controlled Double Blind Cross-Over Investigation of the Side Effects Attributed to Oral Contraceptives." *Fertility and Sterility* 22, 9 (September, 1971).

Goldzieher, J.W., Moses, L.E., and Ellis, L.T. "A Field Trial with a Physiologic Method of Conception Control," in C.V. Kiser (ed.) *Research in Family Planning*. Princeton: Princeton University Press, 1962.

Goodman, L.S. "The Problems of Drug Efficacy: An Exercise in Dissection," in P. Talalay (ed.) *Drugs in Our Society*. Baltimore, Maryland: The Johns Hopkins Press, 1964.

Goodrich, W.W. "The Responsibilities of Government," in P. Talalay (ed.) *Drugs in Our Society*. Baltimore, Maryland: The Johns Hopkins Press, 1964.

Gould, D. "Pill and Thrombosis." *New Statesman* 73 (April 14, 1967).

Graubard, S.R. Preface to the issue, *Ethical Aspects of Experimentation with Human Subjects, Daedalus* (Spring, 1969).

Greenwald, Peter. "Expert on Cancer Wary of New Pill – Plan for DES Contraceptive is Dangerous, Panel Told." *New York Times* (February 23, 1973).

Greenwald, P., et al. "Vaginal Cancer After Maternal Treatment with Synthetic Estrogens." *The New England Journal of Medicine* 285 (August 12, 1971).

Halbert, D.R. and Christian, C.D. "Amenorrhea Following Oral Contraceptives." *Obstetrics and Gynecology* 34, 2 (1969).

Harris, E.L. "Aspects of the Safety of Medicines." *Rheumatol. Phys. Med.* 11 (November, 1972).

Harris, R. *The Real Voice*. New York: The Macmillan Co., 1964.

Hastings Center. "Physical Manipulation of the Brain." Special Supplement (May, 1973).

————. *Values, Expertise, and Responsibility in the Life Sciences* 1, 2 (1973).

Hastings Law Journal. "Liability of Birth Control Pill Manufacturers." *Hastings Law Journal* 23 (May, 1972).

Hatcher, R.A. and Conrad, C.C. "Adenocarcinoma of the Vagina and Stilbestrol as a 'Morning-After' Pill." Correspondence in *The New England Journal of Medicine* 285, 22 (November 25, 1971).

Hauser, P.M. and Duncan, O.D. (eds.) "The Nature of Demography," in *The Study of Population, An Inventory and Appraisal*. Chicago: University of Chicago Press, 1969.

Health Research Group. *Report on the Morning-After Pill*. (December 8, 1972).

Hefnawi, F.E. "Four Years Field Study with Oral Contraception in Egypt," in *Social and Medical Aspects of Oral Contraception*, Round Table Conference. Excerpta Medica Foundation: Scheveningen, The Netherlands (May 1, 1966).

Herbst, A., Ulfelder, H. and Poskanzer, D.C. "Adeno-carcinoma of the Vagina." *The New England Journal of Medicine* 284, 16 (April 22, 1971).

Hertz, R. and Bailer, J.C., III. "Estrogen-Progestogen Combinations for Conception." *Journal of the American Medical Association* 198, 9 (November 28, 1966).

Hiersche, H.D., Hiller, C. and Friedberg, V. "Birth Control. Moral, Theological, Medico-Gynecologic and Penal Aspects." *Geburtsh Frauenheilk* 30 (April, 1970).

Hill, A.B. "Diseases of Treatment." *Public Health* 85 (July, 1971).

Himes, N.E. *Medical History of Contraception.* New York: Schocken Books, 1970.

Inglis, B. *Drugs, Doctors and Disease.* London, England: Andre Deutsch, 1965.

Inman, W.H.W. and Vessey, M.P. "Investigation of Deaths from Pulmonary, Coronary and Cerebral Thrombosis and Embolism in Women of Child-Bearing Age." *British Medical Journal* 2 (1968).

International Planned Parenthood Federation. "Animal Tests Suggest No Cancer Risk for the Pill." *International Planned Parenthood Federation Medical Bulletin* 6, 6 (December, 1972).

———. "Is the Pill Getting Safer?" *International Planned Parenthood Federation Medical Bulletin* 6, 3 (1972).

———. *A Survey of the Legal Status of Contraception, Sterilization and Abortion in European Countries.* London: March, 1973.

Ithaca Journal. "Pill Is Blamed in $7-Million Suit." *Ithaca Journal* (April 9, 1973).

Jaffe, L.L. "Law as a System of Control." *Daedalus* (Spring, 1969): 411.

Jones, G.W. and Mauldin, W.P. "Use of Oral Contraceptives: With Special Reference to Developing Countries." *Studies in Family Planning* 24. New York: The Population Council, December, 1967.

Journal of the American Medical Association. "Common Law and Clinical Investigation." *Journal of the American Medical Association* 203 (February, 1968).

———. "Fertility Control — When." *Journal of the American Medical Association* 214 (December 7, 1970).

———. "A Pox on the Pill." *Journal of the American Medical Association* 213 (August 31, 1970).

Journal of the Kansas Medical Society. "Legal Risks in Selling or Prescribing 'The Pill'." *Journal of the Kansas Medical Society* 72 (January, 1971): 37-38.

Kates, R.B., Goss, D.A., and Townes, P.J. "Immediate Postpartum Use of Sequential Oral Contraceptive Therapy." *Southern Medical Journal* 62, 6 (1969).

Keller, A. "Mexico City: A Clinic Dropout Study." *Studies in Family Planning* 2, 9. New York: The Population Council, 1971.

Kelsey, F. *Clinical Investigation in Medicine: Legal, Ethical and Moral Aspects.* Boston University Law-Medicine Research Institute, 1963.

Kistner, R.W. "The Pill on Trial." *American Journal of Obstetrics and Gynecology* 109 (April 15, 1971).

Kistner, R.W. *The Pill.* New York: Delacorte, 1969.

BIBLIOGRAPHY

Klopper, A. "Advertisement and Classification of Oral Contraceptives." *British Medical Journal* 5467 (October 16, 1965).

Kohlhaas, M. "The Prescription of So-Called 'Anti-Baby Pills' from the Legal Viewpoint." *Deutsch Med. WSCHR.* 89 (August 7, 1964).

Kora, S.J. "Effect of Oral Contraceptives on Lactation." *Fertility and Sterility* 20, 3 (1969).

Kunin, C.M., McCormack, and Abernathy, J.R. "Oral Contraceptives and Blood Pressure." *Archives of Internal Medicine* 123, 4 (1969).

Kutner, J.S. "A Test for Fear of Pregnancy and its Relation to Oral Contraceptives." *Journal of Psychiatric Research* 9 (1972).

Lancet. "A Case to Consider." *Lancet* 1 (March 13, 1971).

————. "Birth Control." *Lancet* II (1963).

Lasagna, L. *The Doctor's Dilemmas.* New York: Harper and Brothers Publishers, 1962a.

————. *Life, Death, and the Doctor.* New York: Knopf, 1968.

————. "On Evaluating Drug Therapy: The Nature of the Evidence," in P. Talalay (ed.) *Drugs in Our Society.* Baltimore, Maryland: The Johns Hopkins Press, 1964.

————. "The Quantification of Desired and Undesired Effects of Reproductive Controls: Some Principles and Problems," in M.C. Sheps and J.C. Ridley (eds.) *Public Health and Population Change – Current Research Issues.* Pittsburgh: The University of Pittsburgh Press, 1965.

————. "The Controlled Clinical Trial: Theory and Practice," *Journal of Chronic Diseases,* I (1955).

————. "Controlled Trials: Nuisance or Necessity?" *Methods of Information in Medicine,* I (1962b).

Law, B. "The Present State of Oral Contraception." *Medical Gynecology, Andrology and Sociology* 6 (November/December 1972).

Lee, L.T. "Law and Family Planning." *Studies in Family Planning* 2, 4 (New York: The Population Council, April, 1971).

————. "Law, Human Rights and Population: A Strategy for Action." *United Nations Economic Commission for Asia and the Far East.* Tokyo, Japan: Second Asian Population Conference. November 1972.

Lee, L.T. and Larson, A. (eds.) *Population and Law.* Durham, North Carolina: Rule of Law Press, 1971.

Lessing, L. "Laws Alone Can't Make Drugs Safe." *Fortune* (March, 1963).

Levin, R., Jowett, A.I. and Raffan, A.G. "Conception Control in Doctors' Families." *Practitioner* 204 (May, 1970).

Liddle, G.G. "Birth Control by the FDA." *Journal of the American Medical Association* 212 (April 6, 1970).

Linden, George, M.P.H. and Henderson, Brian E., M.D. "Genital Tract Cancers in Adolescents and Young Adults." *New England Journal of Medicine* 286, 11 (April 6, 1972).

Loraine, J.A. and Bell, E.T. *Fertility and Contraception in the Human Female.* Edinburgh: E. & S. Livingstone Ltd., 1968.

MacDonald, A. "Angles on the Ethics of Medicines." *Crucible* (November, 1967).

Mahoney, T. *The Merchants of Life.* New York: Harper and Brothers, 1959.

Mamdani, M. *The Myth of Population Control — Family, Caste, and Class in an Indian Village.* New York: Monthly Review Press, 1972.

Markham, J.W. "Economic Incentives and Progress in the Drug Industry," in P. Talalay (ed.) *Drugs in Our Society.* Baltimore, Maryland: The Johns Hopkins Press, 1964.

Marx, J. "Birth Control: Current Technology, Future Prospects." *Science* 179 (March 23, 1973).

Mastroianni, L., Jr. "Safety of Oral Contraception." *Fertility and Sterility* 21 (March, 1970).

Mendelsohn, E., Swazey, O.P. and Taviss (eds.) *Human Aspects of Biomedical Innovation.* Cambridge, Massachusetts: Harvard University Press, 1971.

Miller, R.W. "Transplacental Chemical Carcinogenesis in Man." *Journal of the National Cancer Institute* 17, 6 (December, 1971).

Mintz, M. *The Pill: An Alarming Report.* Boston: Beacon Press, 1970.

————. *"The Therapeutic Nightmare.* (Boston: Houghton Mifflin Co., 1965.

————. "The Golden Pill." *New Republic* (March 2, 1968).

Moore, F. D. "Therapeutic Innovation: Ethical Boundaries in the Initial Clinical Trials of New Drugs and Surgical Procedures." *Daedalus* (Spring, 1969).

Morris, R.D. and Moritz, A.R. *Doctor and Patient and the Law,* 5th ed. Saint Louis: The C.V. Mosby Company, 1971.

Moss, G.E. *Illness, Immunity and Social Interaction.* New York: John Wiley and Sons, 1973.

Mueller, M. "The Pill Doesn't Poison." *Science* 1964 (April 4, 1969).

Naess, K. "Responsibility for Adverse Drug Effects." *Tidsskr Nor Laegeforen* 91 (March 30, 1971).

National Science Foundation. *Interactions of Science and Technology in the Innovative Process: Some Case Studies,* Final Report/NSF-6667 (March 19, 1973).

Nation's Health. "FDA Bans Implanting of DES in Beef Cattle." *The Nation's Health* (June, 1973): 4.

Nelkin, D. *Methadone Maintenance: A Technological Fix.* New York: George Braziller, 1973.

Nelson, W.O. "Current Research on New Contraceptive Methods," in M.C. Sheps and J.C. Ridley (eds.) *Public Health and Population Change, Current Research Issues.* Pittsburgh: The University of Pittsburgh Press, 1965.

New York Times. "The Birth Pill Dispute." *New York Times* (February 23, 1973).

————. "Expert on Cancer Wary of New Pill." *New York Times* (February 23, 1973).

Noel, Dix W. "Products Defective Because of.Inadequate Directions or Warnings." *23 Sw. L.J. 256* (1969).

Okrent, S. *A Clinical Guide to Oral Contraception.* Wantagh, New York: Okrent, 1971.

Onieal, M. "Women are Guinea Pigs for Morning-After Pill." *Syracuse New Times* (February 23, 1973).

Ortiz, E.M. "Current View of the Food and Drug Administration on

BIBLIOGRAPHY

Oral Contraceptives." *Journal of Reproductive Medicine* 7 (July, 1971).

Parsons, T. "Some Theoretical Considerations Bearing on the Field of Medical Sociology," in *Social Structure and Personality*. Glencoe Free Press, 1964.

————. "Research with Human Subjects and the 'Professional Complex'." *Daedalus* (Spring, 1969).

Paul, Michael A. "The Pill — A Legal and Social Dilemma." *Temple Law Quarterly* 45 (Spring, 1972).

Paulsen, C.A. "Oral Contraceptives — Turmoil and Aftermath." *Journal of the American Medical Association* 212 (May 4, 1970).

Perez, V., Gorosdisch, S., deMartise, J. et al. "Oral Contraceptives: Long-Term Use Produces Fine Structural Change in Liver Mitochondria." *Science* 165 (1969).

Pharmaceutical Manufacturers Association. *PMA Newsletter* 15, 19 (May 11, 1973).

————. "FDA Defends Policy on IUD Regulation, Urges Passage of Device Legislation." *PMA Newsletter* 15, 22 (June 1, 1973).

Pilpel, H. *Brief Survey of U.S. Population Law*, Law and Population Series, No. 2. Medford, Massachusetts: The Fletcher School of Law and Diplomacy and Population Program, Tufts University, 1971.

Pincus, G. et al. "Effectiveness of Oral Contraceptive: Effects of Progestin-Estrogen Combination Upon Fertility, Menstrual Phenomena, and Health." *Science* 130 (July 10, 1959).

Potter, R.G., Jr. "Birth Intervals: Structure and Change." *Population Studies* 17, 2 (November, 1963).

Records, J.W. "The Pill Controversy." *Southern Medical Journal* 63 (May, 1970).

Richards, D.W. "A Clinician's View of Advances in Therapeutics," in P. Talalay (ed.) *Drugs in Our Society*. Baltimore, Maryland: The Johns Hopkins Press, 1964.

Richter, R.H.H. "Planning of Clinical Trials with Oral Contraceptives." *Social and Medical Aspects of Oral Contraceptives*. Scheveningen, The Netherlands: Excerpta Medica Foundation, May, 1966.

Ryder, N.B. "Time Series of Pill and IUD Use: United States, 1961-1970." *Studies in Family Planning* 3, 10 (New York: The Population Council, October, 1972).

————. "Use of Oral Contraception in the United States, 1965." *Science* 153 (1966).

Ryder, N.B. and Westoff, C.F. "The Pill and the Birthrate, 1960-1965." *Studies in Family Planning* 20 (1967).

Sadusk, J.F., Jr. "Drugs and the Public Safety." *Annals of Internal Medicine* 65 (October, 1966).

Sandberg, E.C., M.D., and Jacobs, R.I., M.D. "Psychology of the Misuse and Rejection of Contraception." *American Journal of Obstetrics and Gynecology* 110, 2 (May, 1971).

Sarason, S.B. *The Creation of Settings and the Future Societies*. San Francisco: Josey-Bass, Inc., 1972.

Sartwell, P.E., Masi, A.T. et al. "Thromboembolism and Oral Contraceptives: An Epidemiological Case-Control Study." *American Journal of Epidemiology* 90 (November, 1969).

Satterthwaite, A.P. "Experience with Oral and Intrauterine Contraception in Rural Puerto Rico," in M.C. Sheps and J.C. Ridley (eds.) *Public Health and Population Change – Current Research Issues.* Pittsburgh: The University of Pittsburgh Press, 1965.

Schaefer, W.V. "Drugs and the Common Law," in P. Talalay (ed.) *Drugs in Our Society.* Baltimore, Maryland: The Johns Hopkins Press, 1964.

Schlesinger, R.B. *Comparative Law,* 3rd ed. Mineola, New York: The Foundation Press, Inc., 1970.

Schmeck, Harold M., Jr. "Lag on Hormone is Laid to FDA." *New York Times* (December 11, 1973).

———. "New Rules Urged for Drug Testing." *New York Times* (May 10. 1973).

Science. "Oral Contraceptives – Government Supported Programs are Questioned." *Science* 163 (February 7, 1969).

Seamon, Barbara. *Free and Female.* New York: McCann & Geoghegan, 1972.

Segal, S.J. "Contraceptive Technology: Current and Prospective Methods." *Reports on Population/Family Planning* 1 (New York: The Population Council, July, 1971).

———. "Contraceptive Research: A Male Chauvinist Plot?" *Family Planning Perspectives* 14, 3 (July, 1972).

Seigel, D., and Corfman, P., M.D. "Epidemiological Problems Associated with Studies of the Safety of Oral Contraceptives." *Journal of the American Medical Association* 203, 11 (March 11, 1968).

Shapiro, S., Schlesinger, E.R. and Nesbit, R.E.L., Jr. *Infant, Perinatal, Maternal, and Childhood Mortality in the United States.* Cambridge, Massachusetts: Harvard University Press, 1968.

Sheps, M.C. and Ridley, J.C. (eds.) *Public Health and Population Change – Current Research Issues.* Pittsburgh: The University of Pittsburgh Press, 1965.

Simmons, H.E. "FDA Looks at the Package Insert." *Food Drug Cosmetic Law Journal* 27 (March, 1972).

Sollitto, S. and Veatch, R.M. *Bibliography of Society, Ethics and the Life Sciences.* New York: The Hastings Center, 1973.

Solomon, J. "Sea of Drugs." *The Sciences* 13, 4 (May, 1973).

South African Medical Journal. "Legal Responsibilities and Liabilities – Intrauterine Contraceptive Devices and Oral Contraceptives, Legal Opinion." *South African Medical Journal* 42 (March 23, 1968).

Southwick, T.P. "FDA Efficiency Drive Stumbles Over the Issue of Drug Efficacy." *Science* 169 (September 18, 1970).

Spellacy, W.N., Buhi, W.C. and Bendel, R.P. "Insulin and Glucose Studies After One Year of Treatment with a Sequential Type Oral Contraceptive." *Obstetrics and Gynecology* 33, 6 (1969).

Starup, J. "A Comparison Between the Efficiency and Side Effects of Oral Contraceptives Using Closely Related Combined and Sequential Preparations." *ACTA Obstetrica Gynecologia Scandanavia* 48, 3 (1969).

Steinfels, Peter. "Confronting the Other Drug Problem." *The Hastings Center Report* 2, 5 (November, 1972): 4-6.

BIBLIOGRAPHY

Streif, R.R. "Folate Deficiency and Oral Contraceptives." Council on Foods and Nutrition 10/70.

Strickland, S.P. *Politics, Science and Dread Disease.* Cambridge, Massachusetts: Harvard University Press, 1972.

Sun, T.H., Chen, F.L. et al. "Taiwan: First Island-Wide Pill Acceptor Follow-up Survey." *Studies in Family Planning* 60 (New York: The Population Council, December, 1970).

Taber, C.W. *Taber's Cyclopedic Medical Dictionary,* 10th ed. Philadelphia: F.A. Davis, Co., 1965.

Talalay, P. (ed.) *Drugs in Our Society.* Baltimore, Maryland: The Johns Hopkins Press, 1964.

Temkin, O. "Historical Aspects of Drug Therapy," in P. Talalay (ed.) *Drugs in Our Society.* Baltimore, Maryland: The Johns Hopkins Press, 1964.

Temple Law Quarterly. "The Pill — A Legal and Social Dillemma." *Temple Law Quarterly* 45 (Spring, 1972).

Theur, R.C. "Effect of Oral Contraceptive Agents on Vitamin and Mineral Needs: A Review." *The Journal of Reproductive Medicine* 8: 1 (January, 1972).

Tietze, C. "The Clinical Effectiveness of Contraceptives." *American Journal of Obstetrics and Gynecology* LXXVIII (1959).

———. "Oral and Intrauterine Contraception: Effectiveness and Safety." *International Journal of Fertility* 13: 4 (October/December, 1968).

———. "Oral Contraceptives and Thromboembolic Disease." *Studies in Family Planning* 25 (New York: The Population Council, December, 1967).

———. "Statistical Assessment of Adverse Experiences Associated with the Use of Oral Contraceptives." *Clinical Obstetrics and Gynecology* 11, 3 (September, 1968).

Titmus, R.M. "Sociological and Ethnic Aspects of Therapeutics," in P. Talalay (ed.) *Drugs in Our Society.* Baltimore, Maryland: The Johns Hopkins Press, 1964.

Tyler, E.T. "Oral Contraception and Venous Thrombosis." *Journal of the American Medical Association* CLXXXV (July 13, 1963).

Tyler, E.T., M.D. "Clinical Use of Oral Contraception," in M.C. Sheps and J.C. Ridley (eds.) *Public Health and Population Change — Current Research Issues.* Pittsburgh: The University of Pittsburgh Press, 1965.

———. "An Oral Contraceptive: 4-Year Study of Norethindrone." *Obstetrics and Gynecology* XVIII (1961).

———. "The Role of the Family Doctor in Family Planning." *Advances in Fertility Control.* Amsterdam: Excerpta Medica Foundation, 1966.

———. (ed.) *Progress in Conception Control 1969.* Philadelphia: J.B. Lippincott Co., 1969.

Tyler, E.T., M.D. and Olson, H.J. "Fertility Promoting and Inhibiting Effects of New Steroid Hormonal Substances." *Journal of the American Medical Association* CLXIX (1959).

Tyler, E.T., M.D. and Holden, A., M.D. "Which Pill for Which Patient?"

Patient Care (February, 1969).

Uhlenbruck, W. "Prescriptions of Drugs to Minors." *Med. Klin.* 67 (February 25, 1972).

United States Advisory Committee on Obstetrics and Gynecology. *Second Report on the Oral Contraceptives.* Washington, D.C.: U.S. Government Printing Office, 1969.

United States House of Representatives. *Regulatory Policies of the Food and Drug Administration.* Hearing of the Subcommittee on Government Operations, 91st Congress, 2nd Session (June 9, 1970).

————. *The British Drug Safety System.* Twenty-second Report by the Committee on Government Operations, 91st Congress, 2nd Session (March 20, 1970).

————. *Prescription Drug Advertising.* Hearing of Subcommittee of the Committee on Government Operations, 91st Congress, 2nd Session (July 17, 1973).

————. *Regulation of Prescription Drug Advertising.* Thirty-ninth Report by the Committee on Government Operations, 91st Congress, 2nd Session (December 10, 1970).

United States Senate. Select Committee on Small Business, *Oral Contraceptives* (Vols. 1-3), *Competitive Problems in the Drug Industry.* Hearing before the Subcommittee on Monopoly, 91st Congress, 2nd Session, Part 15 (January 14, 15, 21, 22, 23, 1970).

Van Keep, P.A., M.D. "The Pill in Figures and Facts." *Advances in Fertility Control* 2, 1 (Amsterdam: Excerpta Medica Foundation, March, 1967).

Veatch, R.M. "'Experimental' Pregnancy." *Hastings Center Report* 1, 1 (June, 1971).

Vessey, M.P. and Doll, R. "Investigation of Relation between Use of Oral Contraceptives and Thromboembolic Disease. A Further Report." *British Medical Journal* 2 (1969).

Viederman, Stephen. "Values, Ethics and Population Education." *The Hastings Center Report* 3, 3(June, 1973): 6-8.

Wade, Nicholas. "AMA Said to Kill Panel to Save Ads." *Science* 179 (February 23, 1973).

————. "DES: A Case Study of Regulatory Abdication." *Science* 177 (July 28, 1972).

————. "Drug Regulation: FDA Replies to Charges by Economists and Industry." *Science* 179 (February 23, 1973).

Walsh, J. "Technological Innovation: New Study Sponsored by NSF Takes Socioeconomic, Managerial Factors Into Account." *Science* 180 (May 25, 1973).

Weil, A. *The Natural Mind: A New Way of Looking at Drugs and the Higher Consciousness.* New York: Houghton Mifflin Co., 1972.

Westoff, C.F. "Experience with Oral Contraception in the United States, 1960-1965." *Clinical Obstetrics and Gynecology* 11 (1968).

————. "The Modernization of U.S. Contraceptive Practice." *Family Planning Perspectives* 4, 3 (July, 1972).

Westoff, C.F., Bumpass, L. and Ryder, N.B. "Oral Contraception, Coital Frequency, and the Time Required to Conceive." *Social Biology* 16 (1969).

BIBLIOGRAPHY

Westoff, C.F. and Ryder, N.B. "Duration of Use of Oral Contraceptives in the U.S., 1960-1965." *Public Health Reports* 83 (April, 1968).

Westoff, L.A. and Westoff, C.F. *From Now to Zero*. Boston: Little, Brown and Company, 1971.

Winter, I.C. "Industrial Pressure and the Population Problem – the FDA and the Pill." *Journal of the American Medical Association* 212 (May 11, 1970).

Wintrobe, M.M. "The Therapeutic Millenium and its Price: Adverse Reactions to Drugs," in P. Talalay (ed.) *Drugs in Our Society*. Baltimore, Maryland: The Johns Hopkins Press, 1964.

World Health Organization. *Developments in Fertility Control*. Report of WHO Scientific Group, No. 424 (Geneva, 1969).

Young, J.H. "Social History of American Drug Legislation," in P. Talalay (ed.) *Drugs in Our Society*. Baltimore, Maryland: The Johns Hopkins Press, 1964.

Zatuchni, G.I., M.D. (ed.) *Postpartum Family Planning – A Report on the International Program*. New York: McGraw-Hill Book Co., 1970.

Zbinden, G. "Drug Safety – Experimental Programs." *Science* 164 (May 9, 1969).

INDEX

INDEX

INDEX